W9-ATH-575

Southern Rooms

ROCKPORT

Southern Rooms

INTERIOR DESIGN FROM MIAMI TO HOUSTON

GLOUCESTER MASSACHUSETTS

ROCKPORT PUBLISHERS

Copyright © 1999 by Rockport Publishers, Inc.
First paperback edition printed in 2002

All rights reserved. No part of this book may be reproduced in any form without written permission of the
copyright owners. All images in this book have been
reproduced with the knowledge and prior consent of
the artists concerned and no responsibility is accepted
by producer, publisher, or printer for any infringe-
ment of copyright or otherwise, arising from the con-
tents of this publication. Every effort has been made to
ensure that credits accurately comply with information
supplied.

First published in the United States of America by:

Rockport Publishers, Inc.
33 Commercial Street
Gloucester, Massachusetts 01930-5089
Telephone: (978) 282-9590
Facsimile: (978) 283-2742
www.rockpub.com

ISBN 1-56496-874-X

10 9 8 7 6 5 4

Design: Fahrenheit
Cover Image: Pat Shanklin/Leo Dowell Interiors, Inc.
Back Cover: Peter Margonelli/Benjamin Noriega Ortiz

Printed in China.

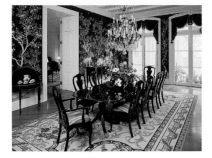

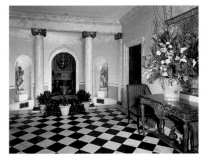

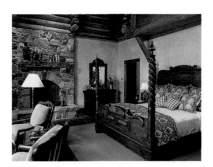

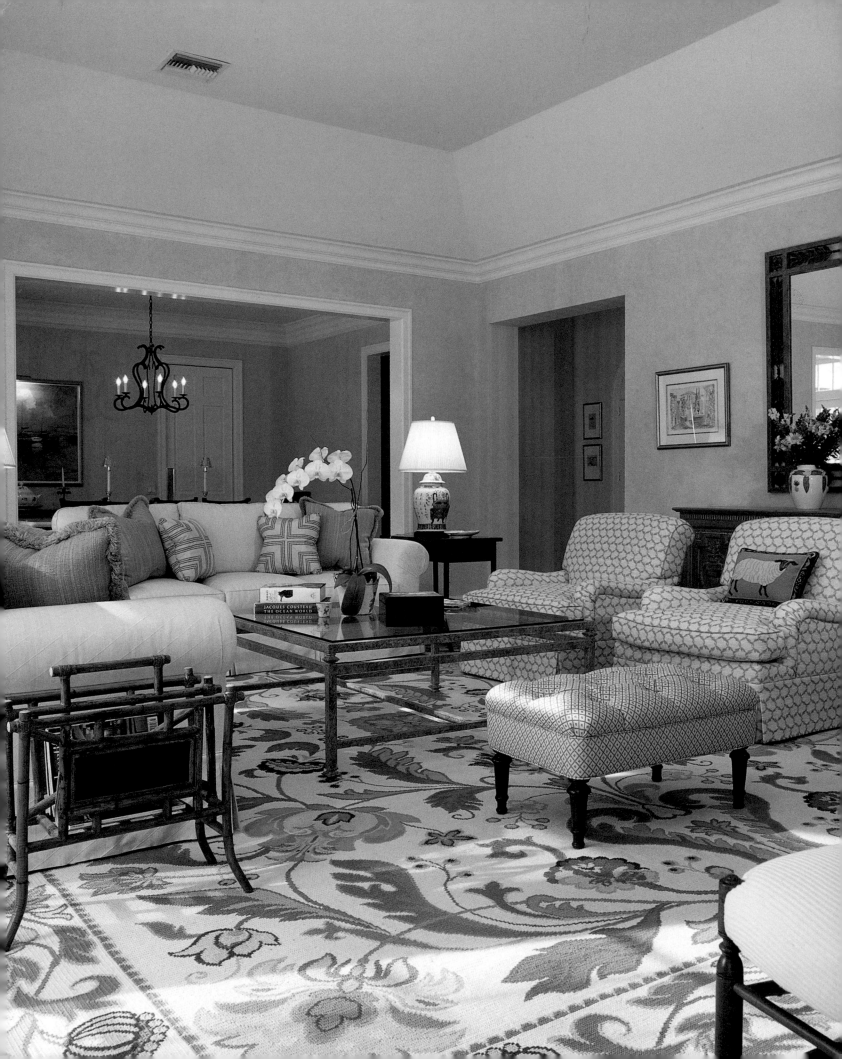

COASTAL
SOUTH

The Coastal South—the sinuous coastline that wraps its way around the peninsula of Florida—has a swagger all its own. In contrast to the formality of the Old South and the derring-do of the New South, the bravado of the Coastal South emerges from a profound sense of its place in history. Florida is home to the oldest European settlement in the United States. Founded in 1565 by the Spanish, St. Augustine preceded Virginia's Jamestown by 42 years. The swashbuckling romance of Florida's early history also gives it a unique position in the annals of American history— just twenty years after Christopher Columbus' first voyage to America, an expedition was already underway to seek a fountain of youth rumored to exist in this new land. We all know that no one ever located the fountain, but it is probably not a coincidence that many thousands of senior citizens have moved to Miami, where sunny days, cool nights, and a soothing ocean breeze is the next best thing.

That ocean breeze is another reason for Florida's vivacity—it brings in fresh scents of the Pacific, but also conjures up lost memories of smells like the decaying timbers of Spanish shipwrecks half-embedded in the waters or tangled gardens of jasmine and honeysuckle flourishing along the chain of barrier islands that stretches around the tip of the state. Here too, the Everglades, the nation's largest subtropical wilderness, keeps primordial secrets of buccaneers and pirates persevering in the search for wealth that the idealistic Spaniards began two centuries earlier.

Cities in Florida reflect that early optimism: Spanish-style architecture, with its rosy pink stucco walls and courtyards, red tile roofs, and rococo ornamentation embellish neighborhoods like a confectioner's fantasy. Along the Keys, whimsical wooden houses, brightly painted and fantastically adorned, attest to the carefree nature of beach-front living. The need for haste and worry seems to have been whisked away by the ocean breeze. Added to these frothy geographical, historical, and architectural rhythms, the glamorous sophistication of the country's largest concentration of Art Deco buildings emphasize the visual extravagance of this region of the South.

Built primarily in the thirties, these buildings symbolize the potent cultural forces at work in Florida: their crowd-pleasing playfulness borrows indiscriminately from futurism, cubism, surrealism and design devices employed by the ancient Assyrians, the Egyptians, the Aztec, and the Mayan cultures as well as the machine esthetic of progressive European designers. You will also see nautical details straight out of the craze for luxury liners—curved walls, circular windows, handrails of tubular metal. Here these streamlined modernist steel, glass, and bright veneer buildings stand almost as sculptures, their tropical, floral, and modern motifs reflecting sleek and anti-traditional elegance, wealth and sophistication.

Florida designers have their own view of the world—and it is a little wilder, a little more iconoclastic, and a little more inventive than everybody else's. Today, even the most elegant and sophisticated interiors will hint at that sense of anti-traditionalism. Here you will see proof of this individualistic approach to design: the offbeat statue, the wildly patterned carpet, and the astonishing chandelier all find the perfect place in houses decorated by the designers in the Coastal South.

[left] *Sunlight streams into this engaging living room, illuminating the apricot-colored glazed walls and patterned rug. The soft glow envelopes the space to make it a very cozy place to entertain guests or simply relax.*

Interior Design: Linda A. Poletti
Interior Decoration, Inc.
Location: Hobe Sound, Florida

CRAWFORD'S INTERIOR DESIGN

Designer Sandy Crawford, ASID, is known for her belief that every client is unique and is deserving of an individual design approach. She successfully creates timeless designs that make each client's project something special. Her designs reflect the client's personality and interests, and as a result enhance their lifestyle through the creation of personal surroundings rich in detail. That philosophy of *something special* transforms residences and offices into elegantly understated rooms with an inviting and comfortable appeal.

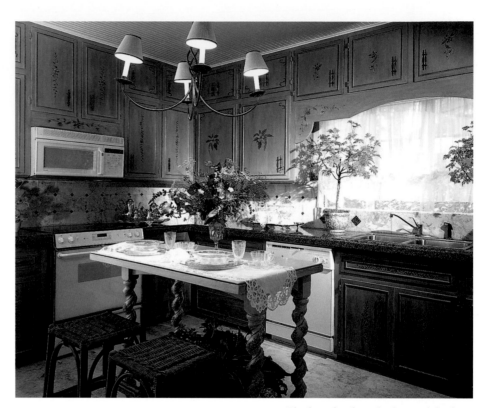

This large farmhouse kitchen needed a face-lift. Existing cabinets were transformed by adding moldings, a wash of color, and a custom-painted design of fruit and flowers. The countertops are pistachio-colored granite and the flooring and backsplash are shell-stone with granite accents.

Location: Orlando, Florida

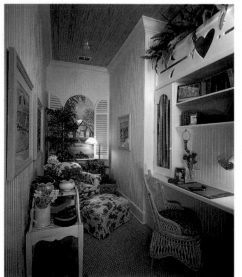

This attractive office was created from a closet in the city of Winter Park Golf Clubhouse. The trompe-l'oiel window is a painting of the house across the street. . . the actual view if there was a window. The beaded board and heart motif repeat the arts-and-crafts details of the original structure.

Location: Winter Park, Florida

[right] *This renovated kitchen encourages a wonderful interchange with the rest of the house. The design inspiration was the rosa verona and botticino tumbled marble. The countertops are a honed rosa-verona slab of marble. The chiseled edges add to the overall aged appearance. The floors are hardwood with painted white wood cabinetry.*

Location: Winter Park, Florida

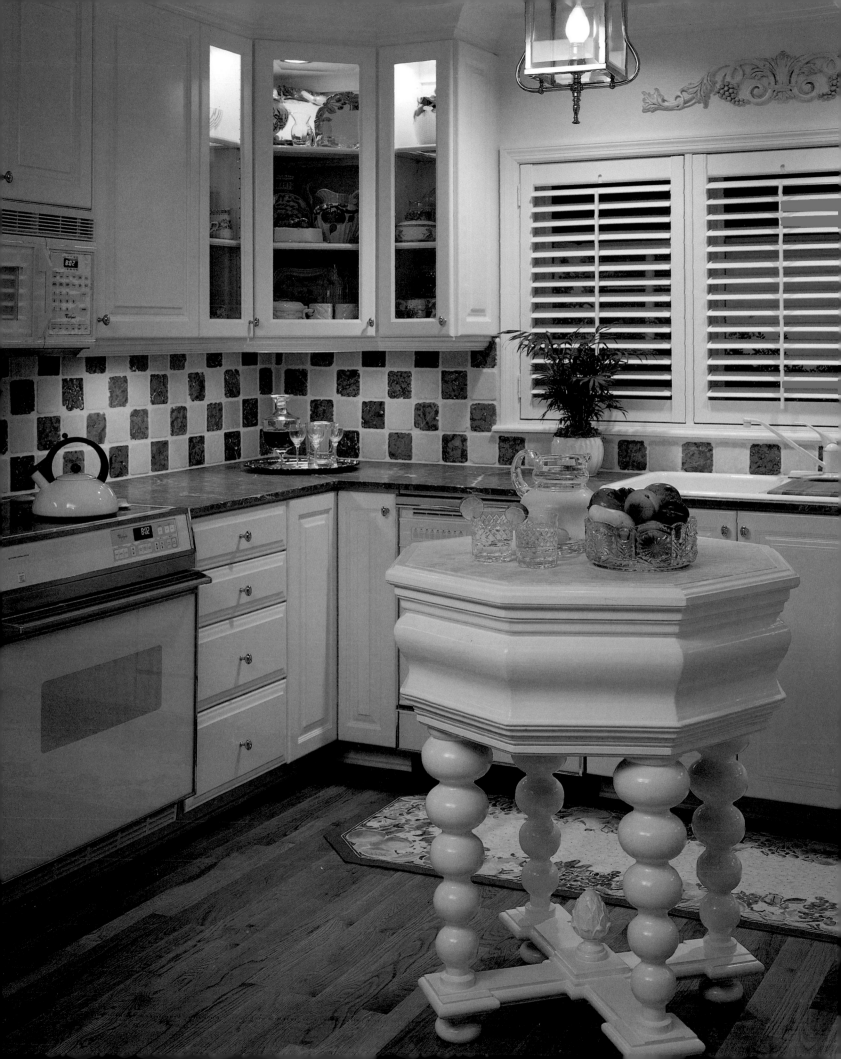

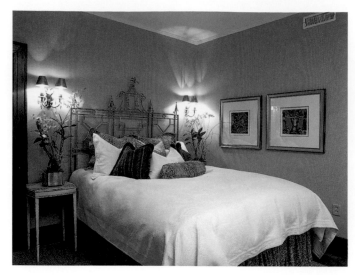

Hardwood floors, seagrass rug, and linen wallcovering add to the restful ambiance of this master bedroom. The bed is a custom chinoiserie design constructed of iron with a hand-applied gold-leaf finish.

Location: Orlando, Florida

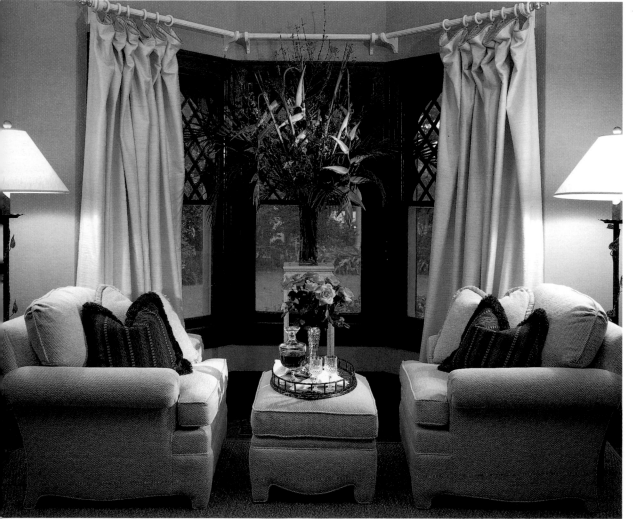

A sitting area in this master retreat was designed for conversation and enjoying the beautiful view of the bay window. The neutral tone-on-tone colors, with a variety of textures and rich tapestries, creates a relaxed mood.

Location: Orlando, Florida

[right] *In this charming nursery, the round crib in the center of the room allows plenty of room to showcase a doll collection and toys for the growing infant. Although not very practical, the giraffe and bunny topiaries were a big hit.*

Location: Orlando, Florida

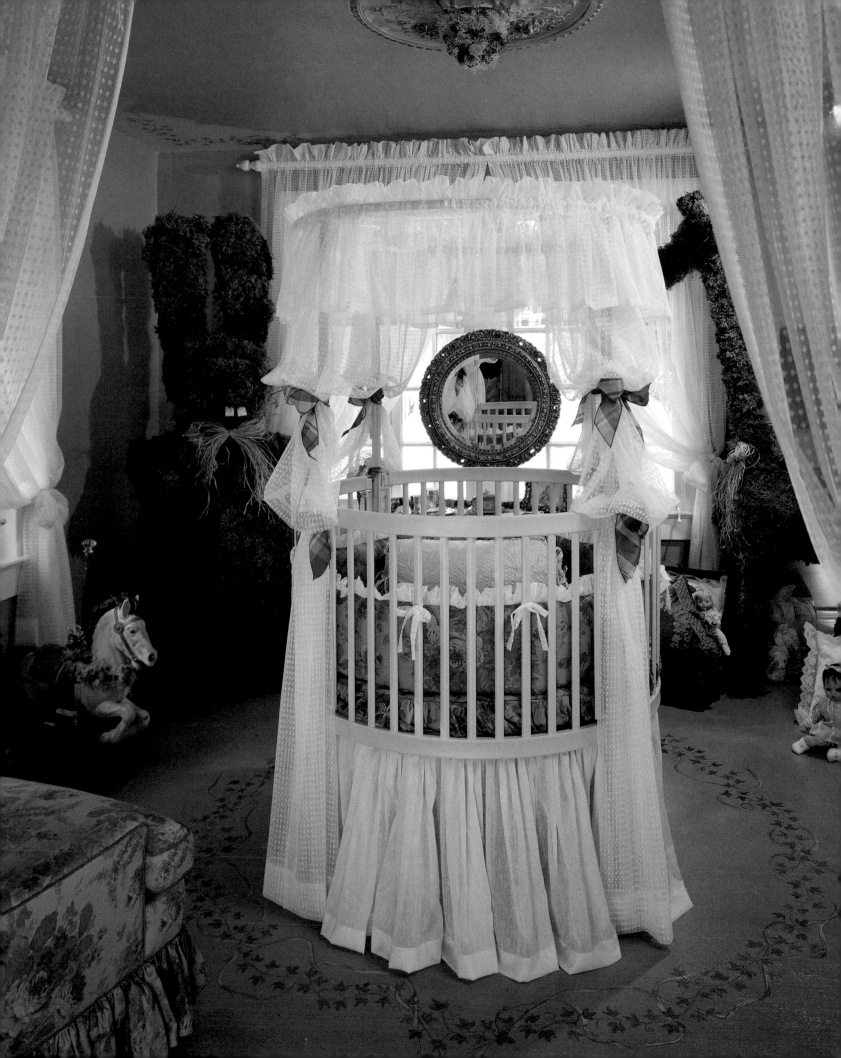

DESIGN EFFECTS

Progressive interpretations of European influences and insistence on unsurpassed quality best exemplify Design Effects' innovative approach to design. The objective is to create timeless works that reflect the spirit and personality of the client.

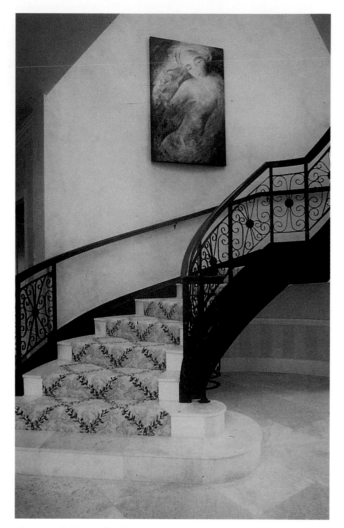

A custom-design needlepoint rug ascends the mahogany stairway. The rug's delicate pattern complements the bold lines of the architecture.

Location: Weston, Florida

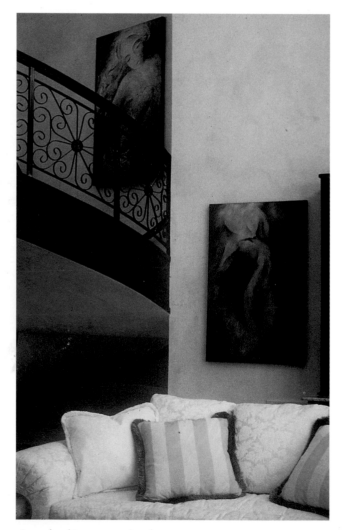

Art and architecture come together gloriously in this elegant space.

Location: Weston, Florida

[right] *Architectural elements establish a mood of relaxed elegance upon entering this home. The grand, iron-laced mahogany stairway imbues the space with a sense of graceful drama.*

Location: Weston, Florida

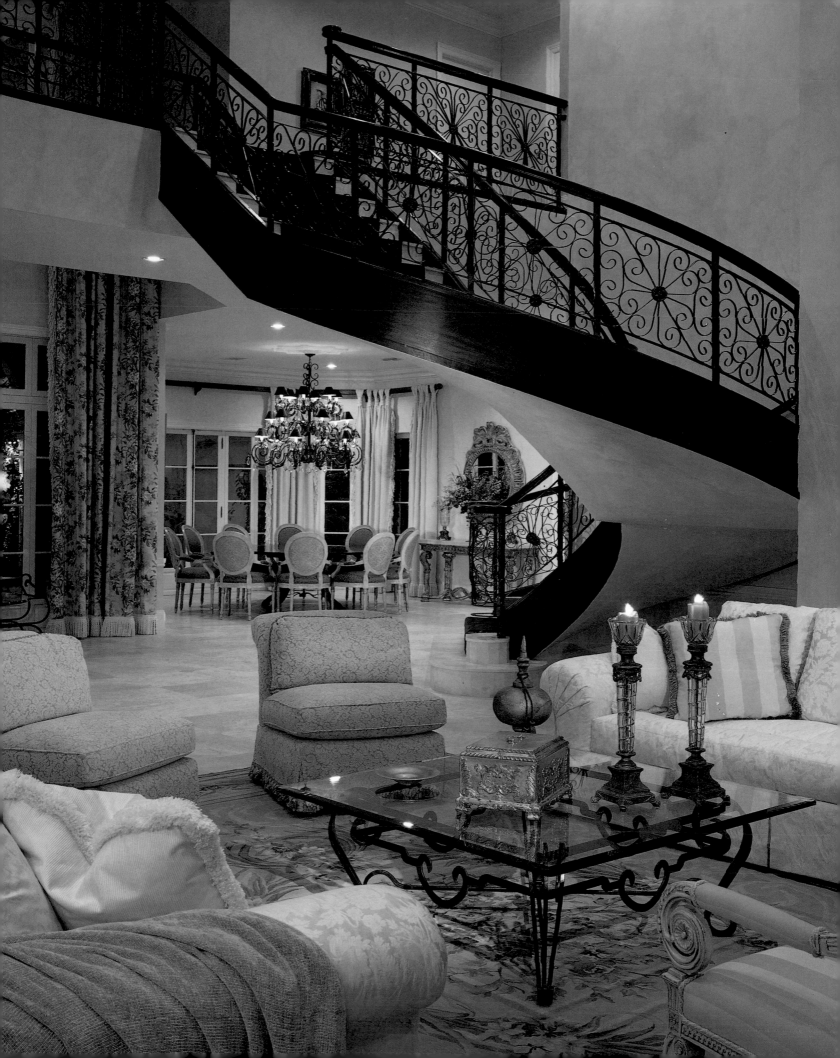

JACK FHILLIPS DESIGN, INC.

Good design should last forever . . . a marriage of the personal style of the designer and the individual style of the client. Rooms should reflect timeless quality and classic design rather than trends and current fashion. Great spaces are like that; they invite living and, over the years, evolve into even greater environments. Age permits interests, and rooms should be an intelligent and stylish representation of those who live in them.

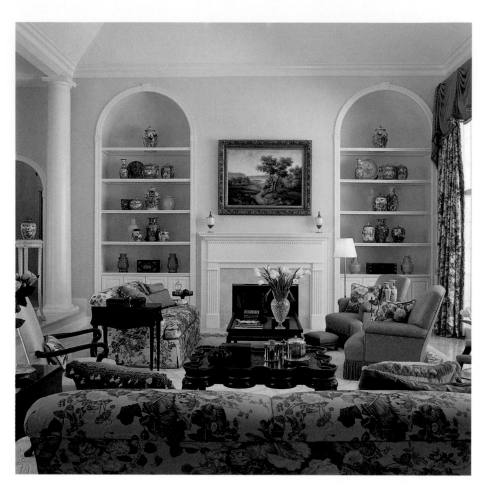

A mix of classical and traditional design elements transforms a voluminous space into an intimate country-English living room. Symmetrical built-in bookcases lend formality.

Location: Palm Beach, Florida

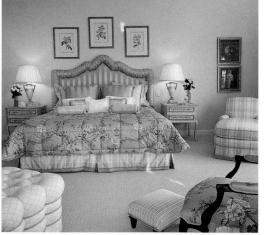

Delicately scaled custom furnishings balanced with antique furnishings instill a delicate sense of elegance in this master bedroom.

Location: Palm Beach, Florida

[right] *This formal living room opens onto an inviting Regency-style foyer and dining room. Furnishings reflect a classic approach to English design.*

Location: Palm Beach, Florida

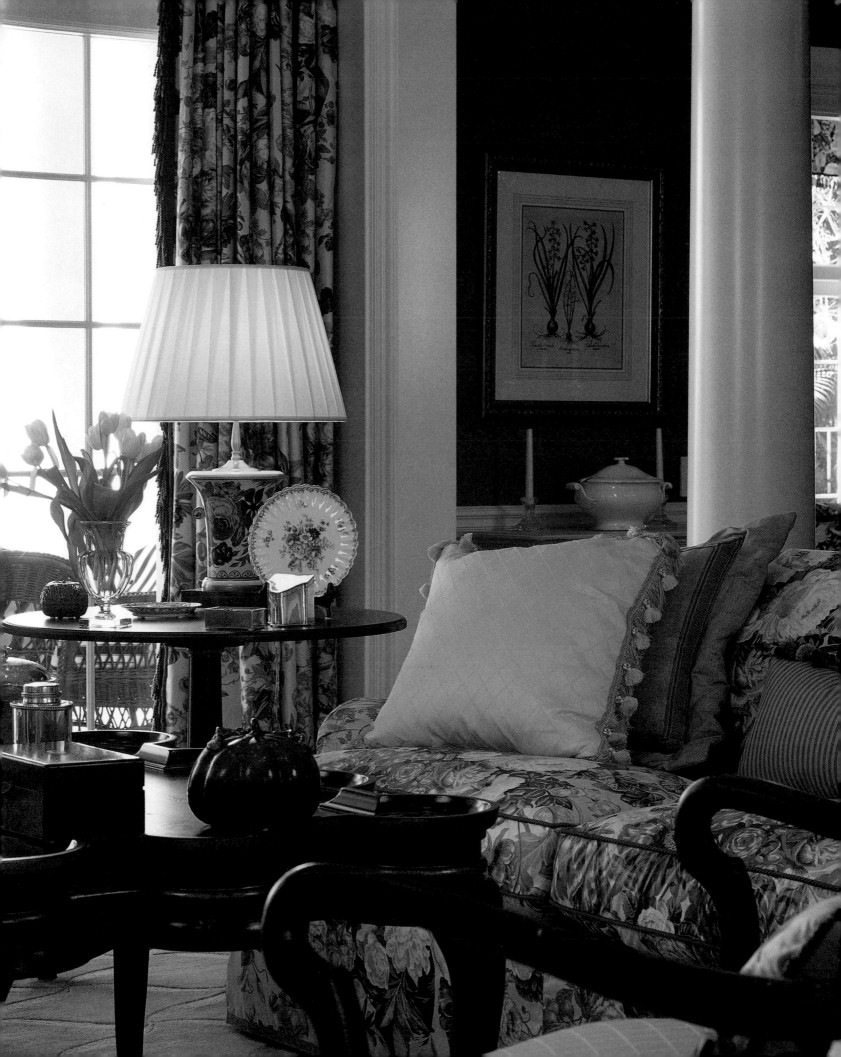

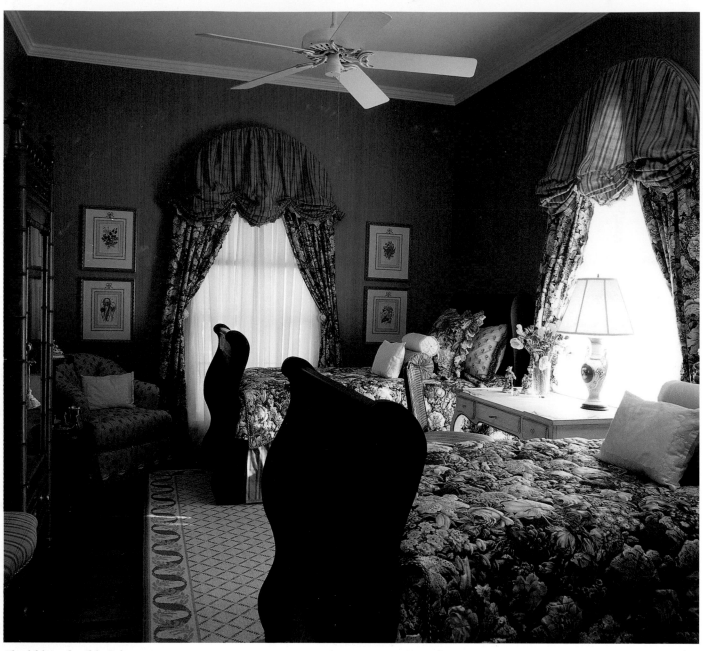

*Floral fabrics, fanciful window treatments,
and a pair of elegant sleigh beds animate
this cozy and comfortable guest bedroom.*

Location: Palm Beach, Florida

[right] *A custom-designed Gothic
headboard crafted of old steel combines with American Empire fur-
nishing and Regency period end
tables to bring classic timelessness to
this guest bedroom.*

Location: Palm Beach, Florida

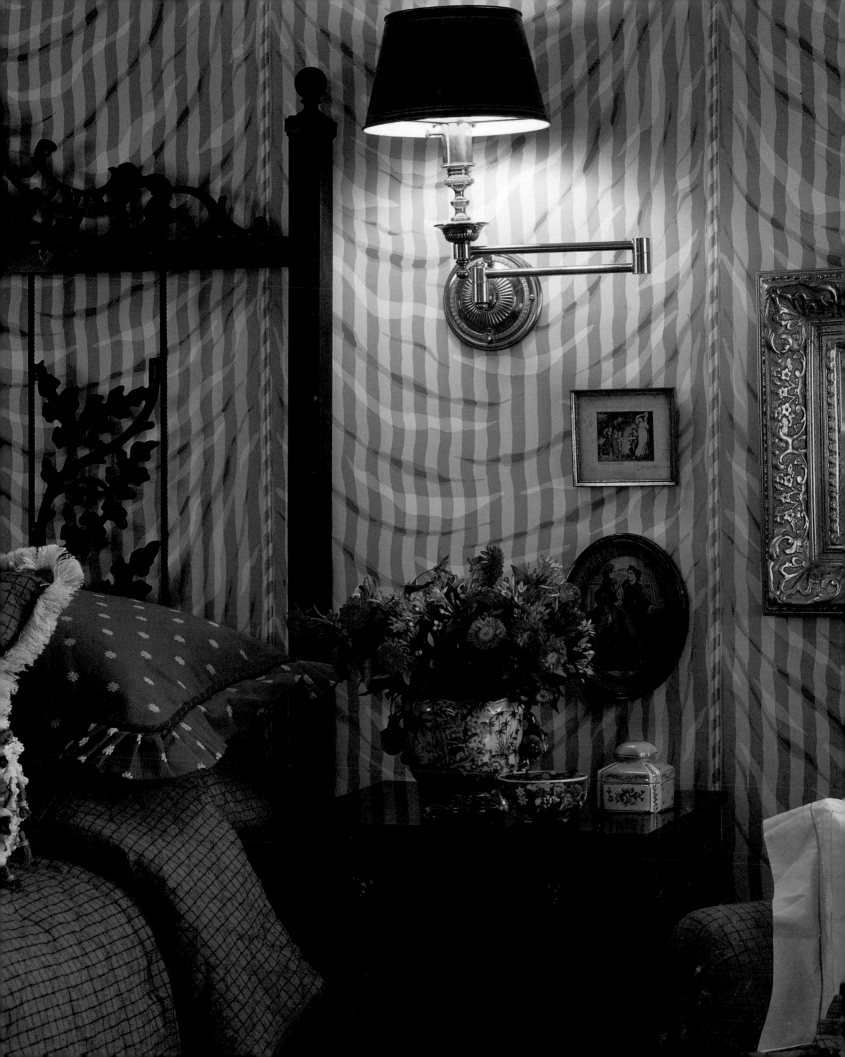

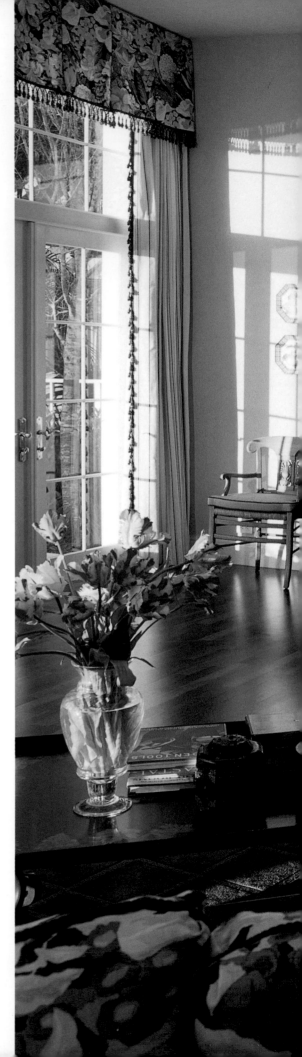

[right] *Sunlight floods through tall windows in this multi-purpose family living area. Furniture placement and refined accessories lend intimacy and comfort to this generous space.*

Location: Palm Beach, Florida

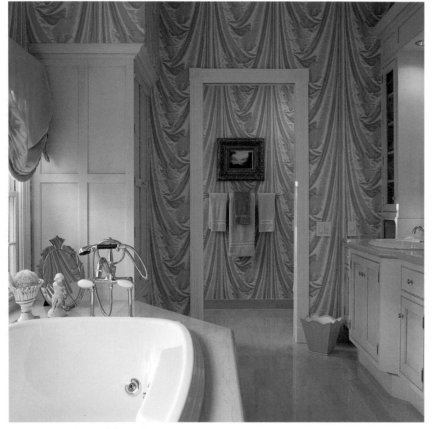

Exquisite detailing and classic design imbue this master bath with comfort and warmth for hours of luxurious relaxation.

Location: Palm Beach, Florida

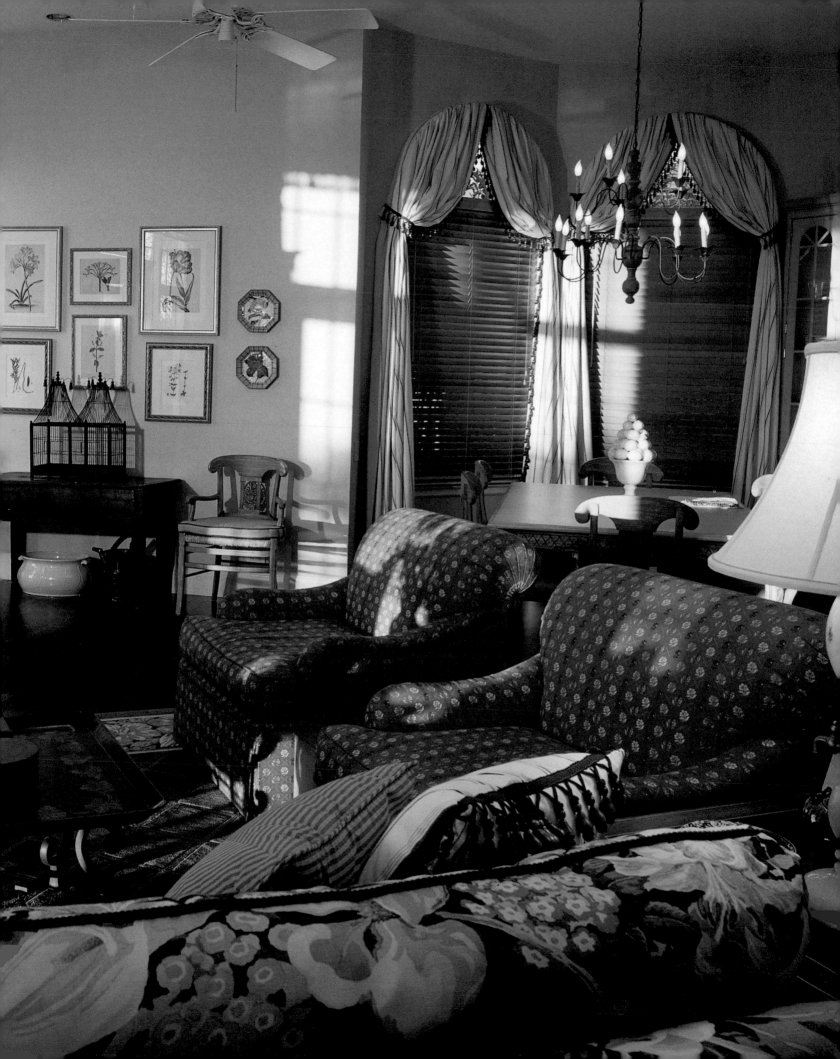

GINNY STINE INTERIORS

Established in 1975, Ginny Stine Interiors provides a full scope of residential and commercial design services. The firm has avoided identifying with one particular style or period, preferring to execute highly individualized solutions. To this end it maintains an extensive resource library with many volumes featuring historic architectural details. Furthermore, they stock an array of period antique furniture, oil paintings, antique engravings, and decorative accessories in their studio located in the charming San Marco district of Jacksonville.

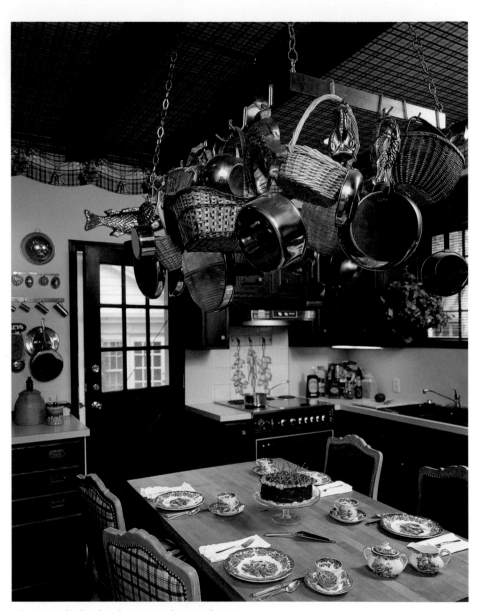

This warm kitchen has the compact elegance of a private rail car. The custom cabinetry is mahogany-stained, raised-panel oak. The hand-painted tiles combine with a distinctive border and ceiling wallpaper to lend old-world charm. The sparkle of the copper and brass cookware adds interest and excitement.

Location: Jacksonville, Florida

[right] *While this living room is large, it maintains a friendly mood through the use of warm color, bright floral fabrics, and a spontaneous furniture arrangement.*

Location: Jacksonville, Florida

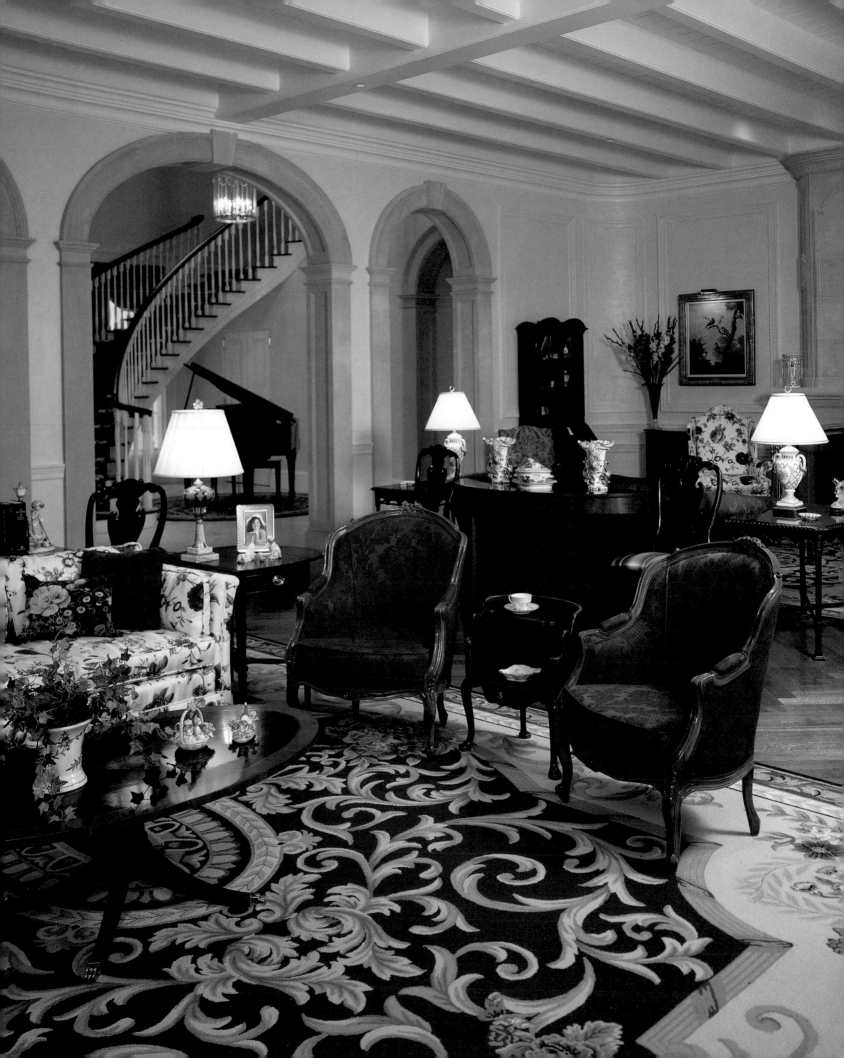

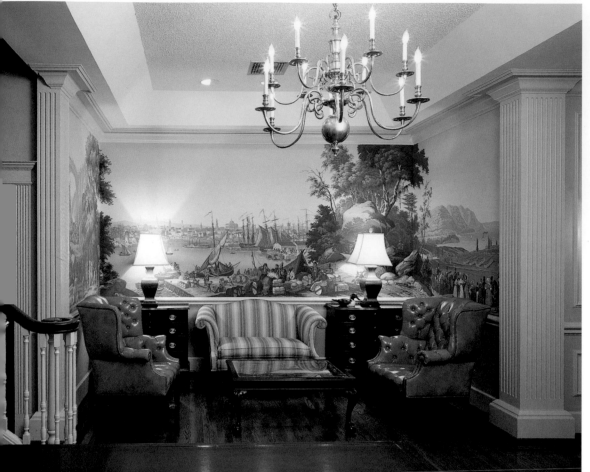

Early nineteenth-century details, including appropriate molding and zuber hand-clocked mural *Scenes of America instill this lobby in a historic restoration project with a sense of authenticity.*

Location: Jacksonville, Florida

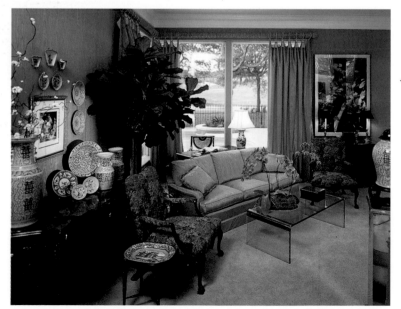

Neutral tones open up this small living room while the antique blue-and-white Chinese porcelains create unity. Black-and-white figural photography adds interest and depth.

Location: Jacksonville, Florida

[right] *This dining room is a modern take on a traditional subject. The Empire inspired chairs are upholstered in a contemporary fabric. The window treatments are made entirely of brass. The gold leaf on the ceiling and walls is repeated in the tablescape, which features traditional tableware.*

Location: Jacksonville, Florida

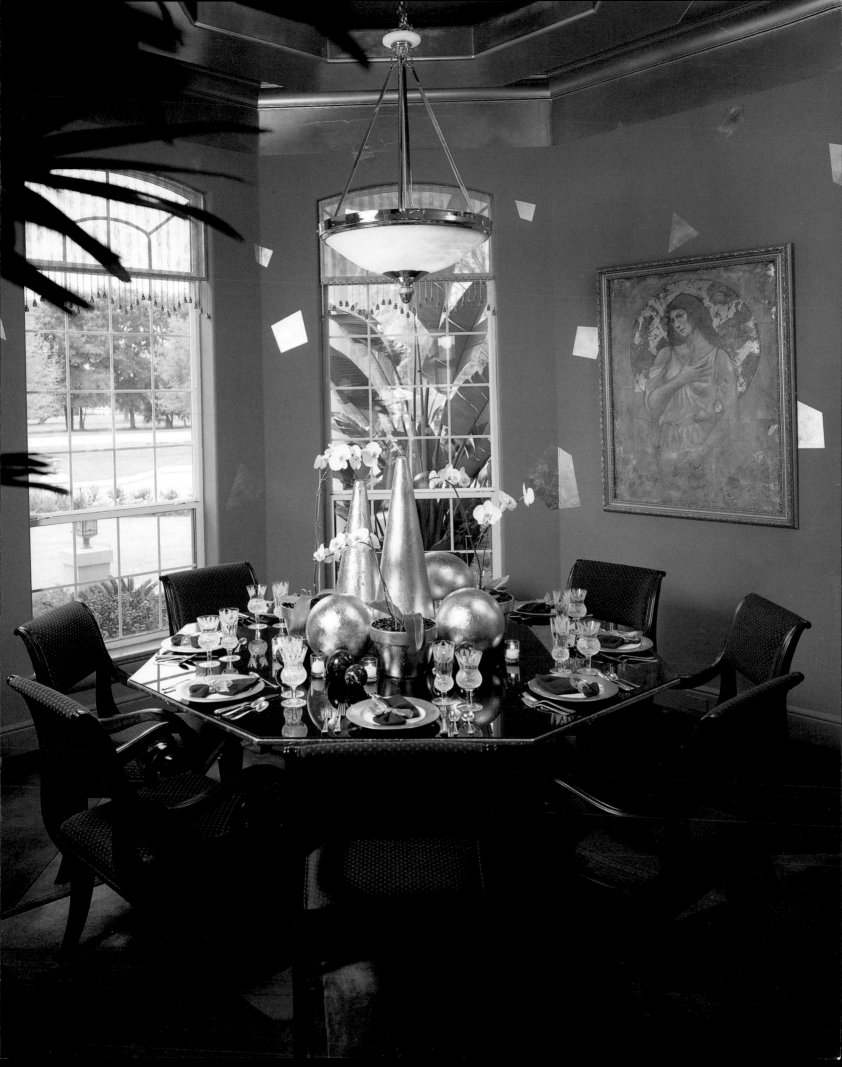

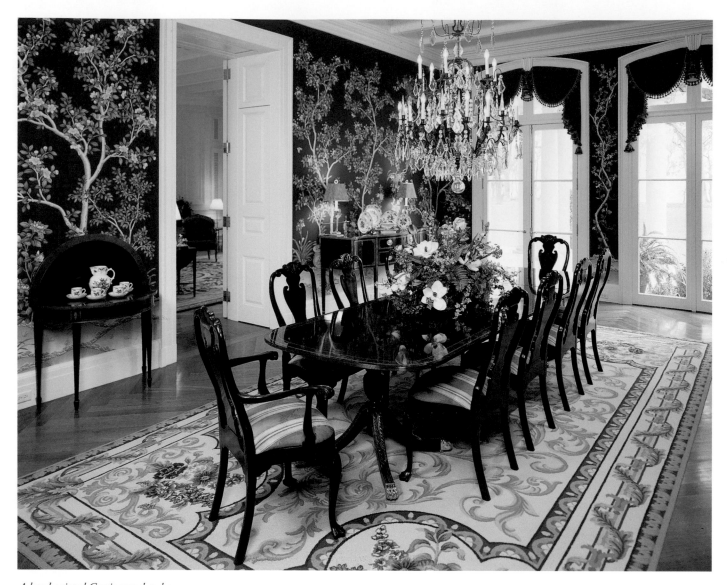

A hand-painted Gracie mural and a custom Lacey Champion carpet lend warmth and character to this long dining room. A bank of floor-to-ceiling arched windows floods the room with natural light.

Location: Jacksonville, Florida

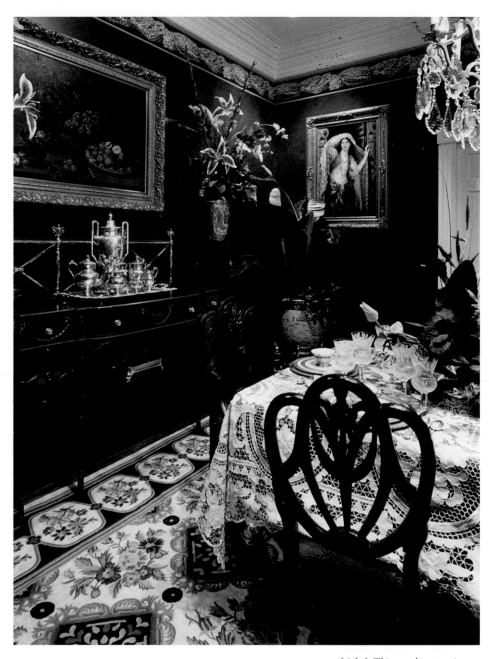

[right] *This moody, mysterious dining room was created to come alive at night. The juxtaposition of exotic florals, paintings, and wallpaper border (zuber) to the elegant English furniture creates a sensational effect.*

Location: Jacksonville, Florida

LINDA A. POLETTI INTERIOR DECORATION, INC.

Taking a simple, refined approach to interior decoration, Linda Poletti incorporates her knowledge of fabrics, antiques, and beautiful objects to create comfortable and intimate interiors. Each detail is carefully selected with the particular space and client in mind. This approach allows each project to appear vastly different in style and formality from another and, more importantly, each project reflects the goals and philosophy of the individual client.

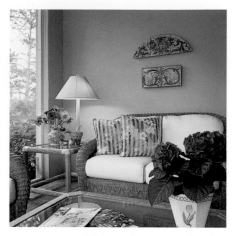

This cheerful sunroom offers the perfect spot for morning coffee all year round. Tall windows offer an inviting interchange between indoors and out.

Location: Hobe Sound, Florida

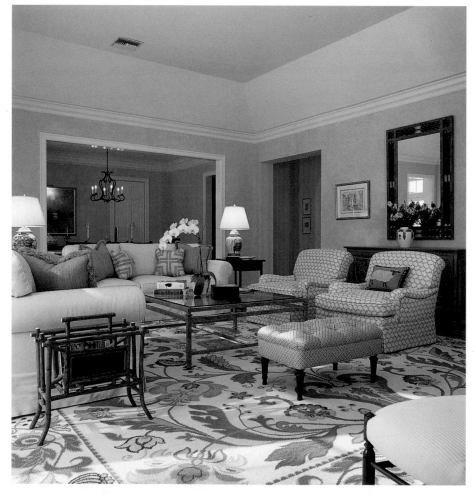

[right] *This comfortable dining room sets a welcoming tone for guests to linger after dinner and chat.*

Location: Hobe Sound, Florida

Sunlight streams into this engaging living room, illuminating the apricot-colored glazed walls and patterned rug. The soft glow envelopes the space to make it a very cozy place to entertain guests or simply relax.

Location: Hobe Sound, Florida

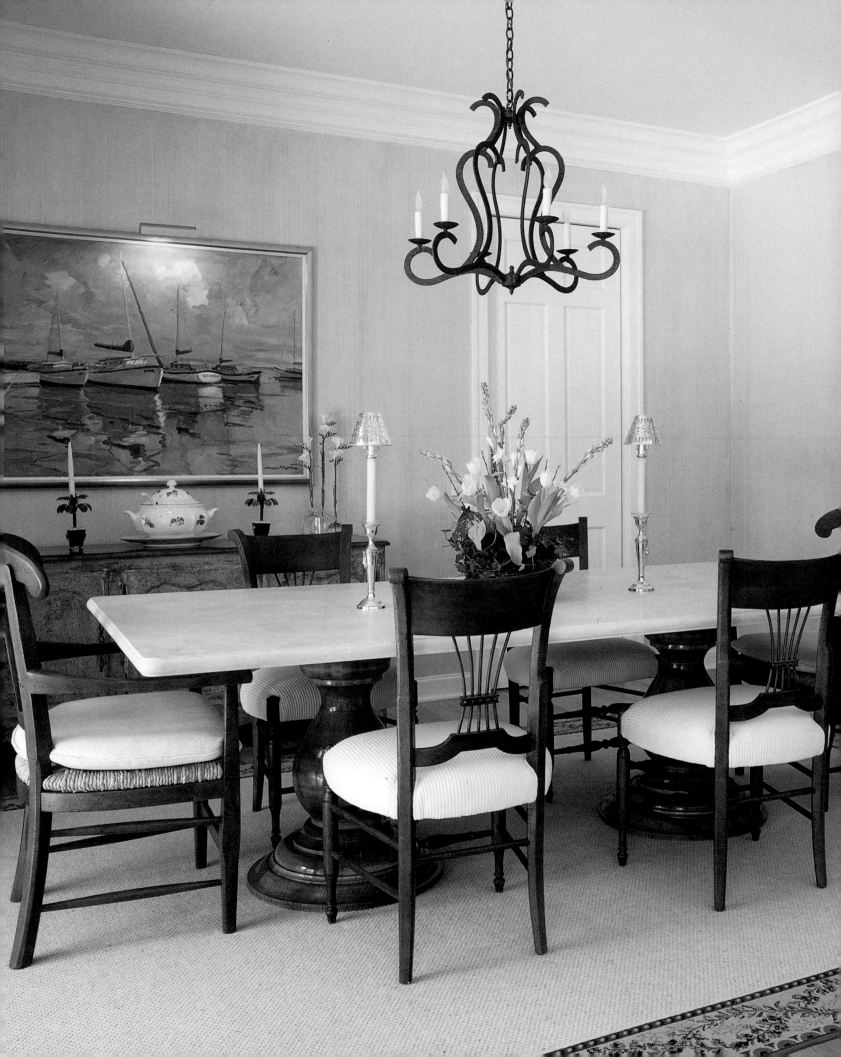

LOVELACE INTERIORS AND CLEMENTS ANTIQUES

Great interior design begins with an understanding of the client's needs. That means each project is unique. A designer must draw on a number of resources: a knowledge of the history of architecture and art, the practical use of fabrics, an eye for detail, and a passion for beautiful things. These talents, combined with a successful collaboration with the client, result in the creation of harmonious, elegant, livable environments with a true sense of timelessness.

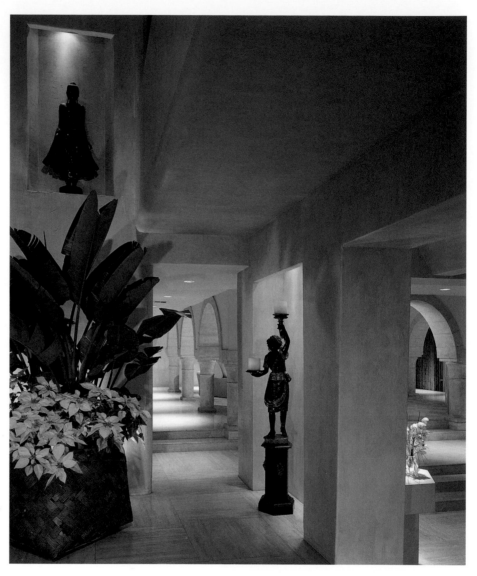

Sliding entry doors recede to reveal one of a pair of rare Venetian blackamoors. These doors that disappear into the walls create sensational sense of progression.

Location: Beverly Hills, California

[right] *An Italian chess set and an English mahogany game table create the perfect environment for frequent entertaining in this distinctive party room.*

Location: Beverly Hills, California

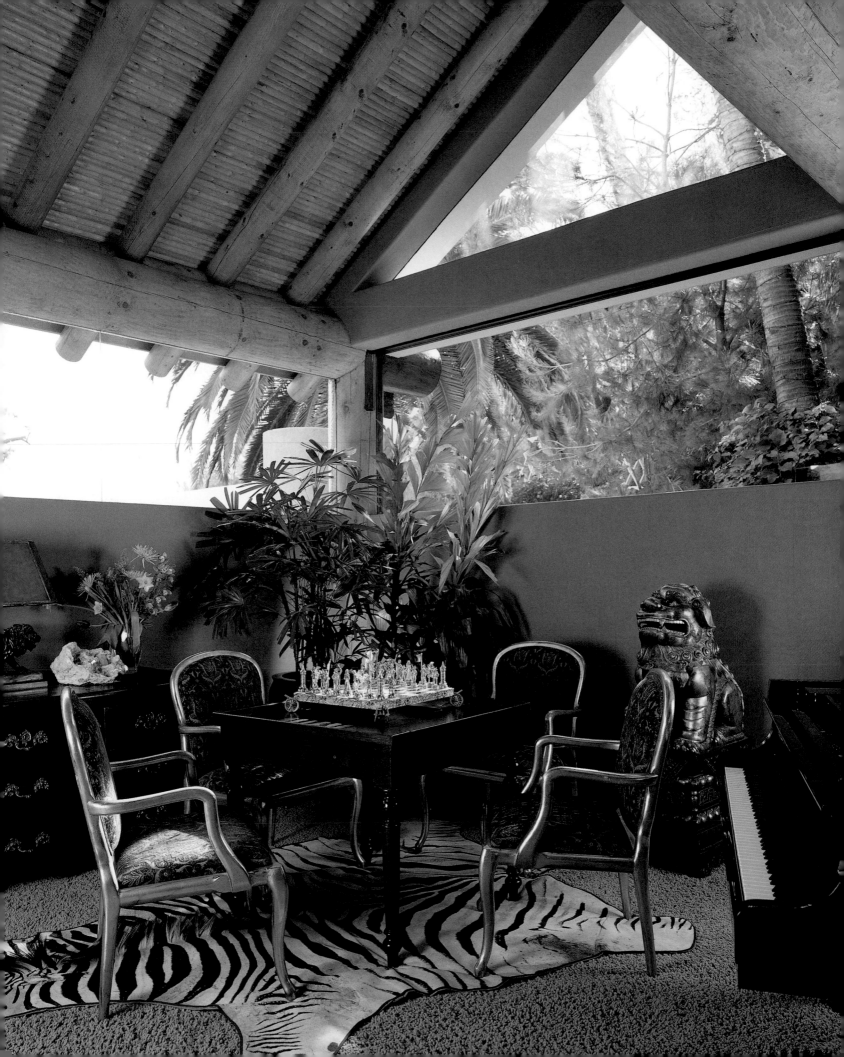

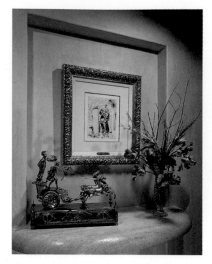

Drama describes the dining hall with its tall gilded walls. The palace-size Louis XVI marble-top console, French gilded mirror, and Venetian black-amoors all date from the mid-nine-teenth century.

Location: Beverly Hills, California

[right] A pair of painted chests frames an iron bed simply dressed with neutral fabrics. The antique French chairs and upholstered chaise lounges add warmth and comfort to this inviting master suite.

Location: Beverly Hills, California

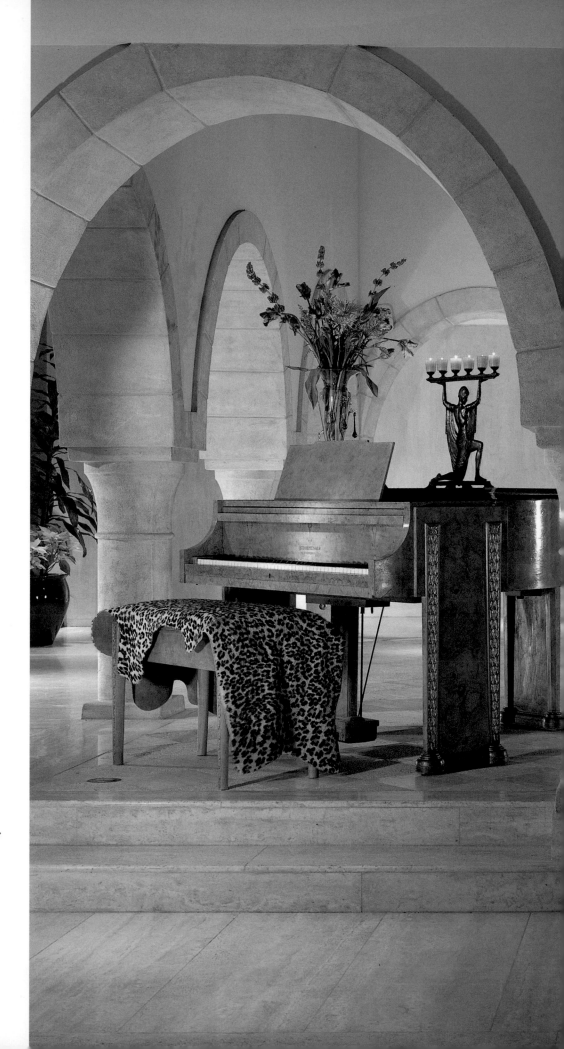

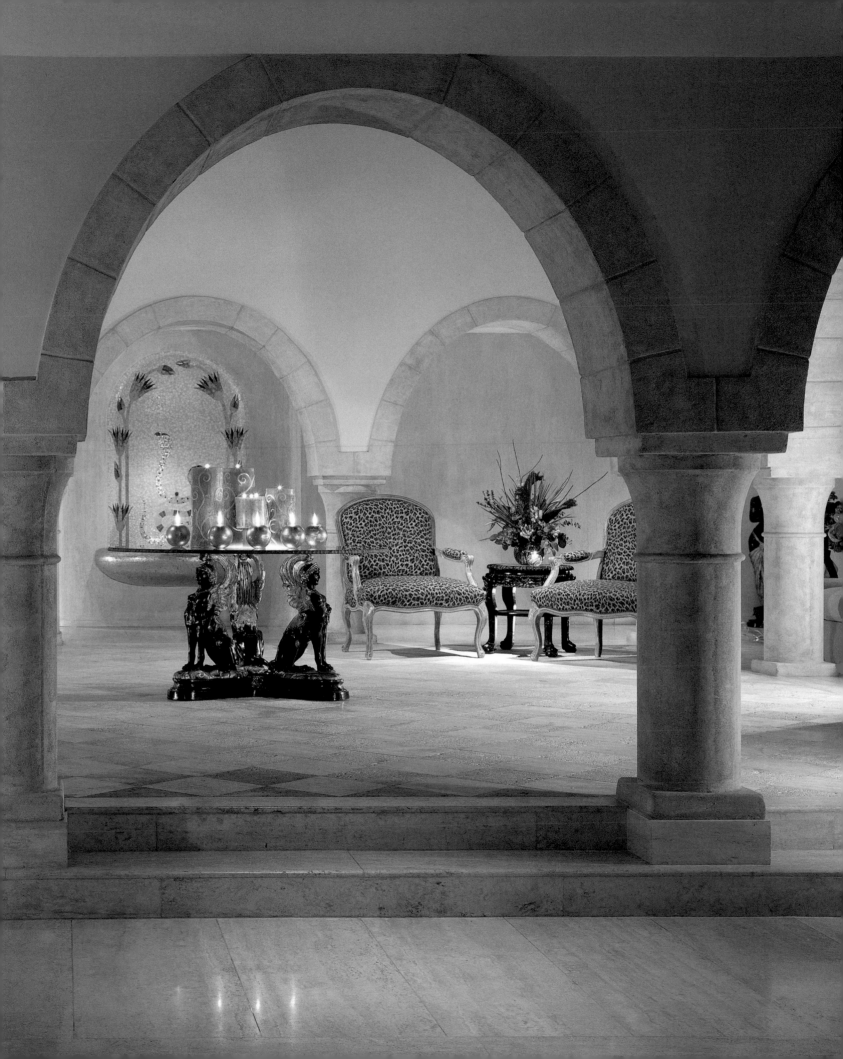

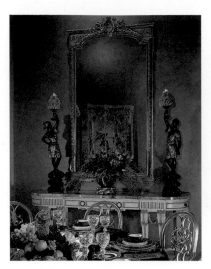

Drama describes the dining hall with its tall gilded walls. The palace-size Louis XVI marble-top console, French gilded mirror, and Venetian black-amoors all date from the mid-nineteenth century.

Location: Beverly Hills, California

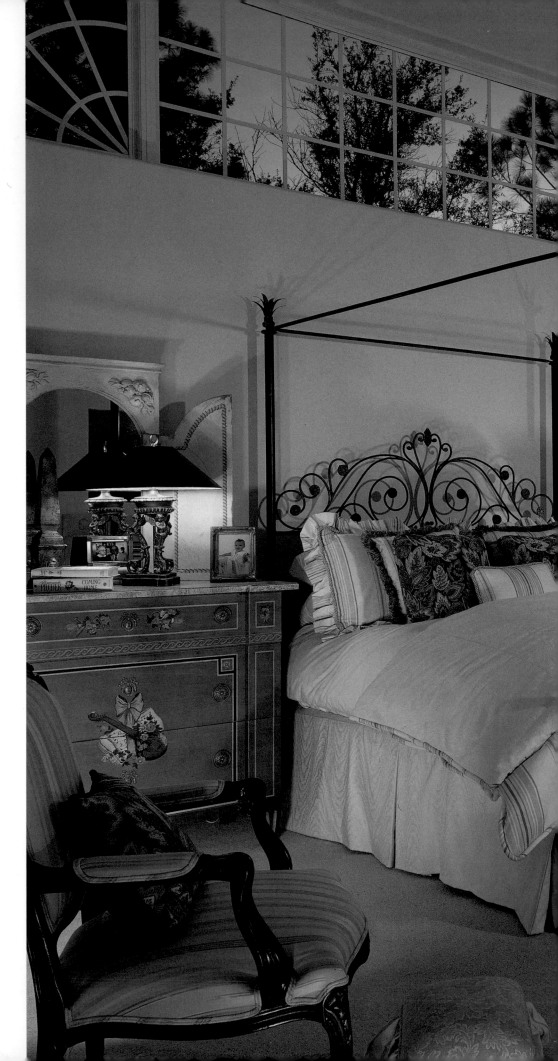

[right] *A pair of painted chests frames an iron bed simply dressed with neutral fabrics. The antique French chairs and upholstered chaise lounges add warmth and comfort to this inviting master suite.*

Location: Beverly Hills, California

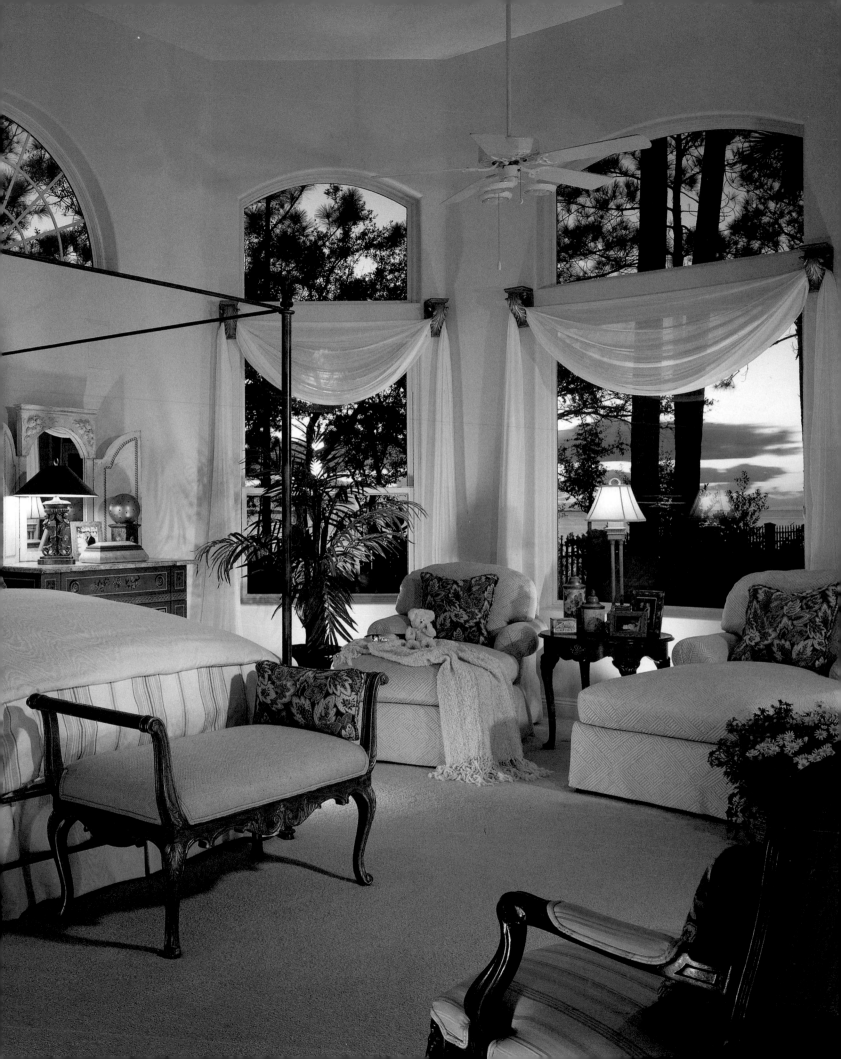

MARC-MICHAELS INTERIOR DESIGN

Regarded as one of the Southeast's most talented interior design firms, Marc-Michaels Interior Design specializes in architectural interiors for yachts, private residences, and commercial projects such as models, clubhouses, and office buildings. Led by Design Principal Marc Thee and CEO Michael Abbott, the staff at Marc-Michaels serves clientele ranging from private clients such as Alan Jackson, Nick Faldo, Gary Player, Jeff Gordon, and Rick Mears to national building companies such as Centex and Arthur Rutenberg Homes. From contemporary to traditional, from lavish to casual, Marc-Michaels Interior Design offers design solutions that are truly memorable in timeless style and spirit.

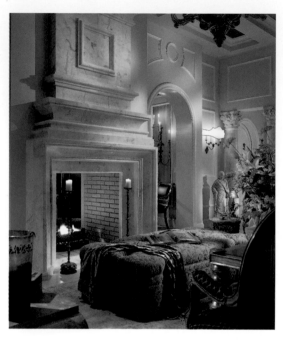

The living room features a hand-carved Mexican shell-stone fireplace, applied moldings, and niches for an original Jamali and antique statue.

Location: Winter Park, Florida

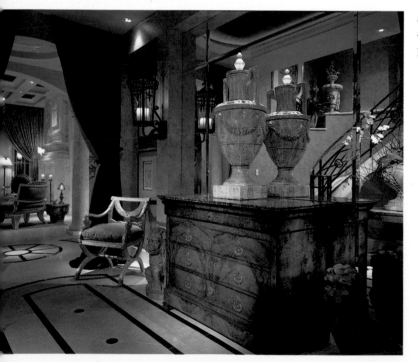

Lush draperies enhance the entryway into the living room.

Location: Winter Park, Florida

[right] *The fully-paneled library acts as a family room also. All the bookshelves are backlit with rope lighting.*

Location: Winter Park, Florida

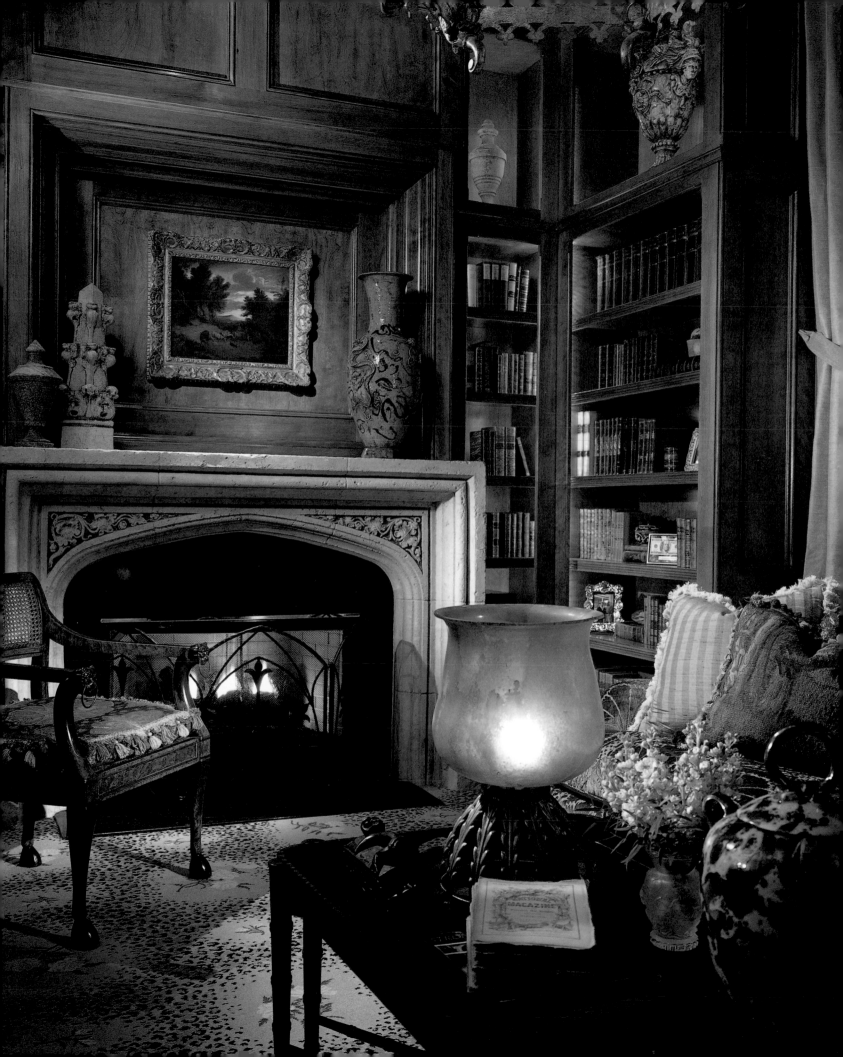

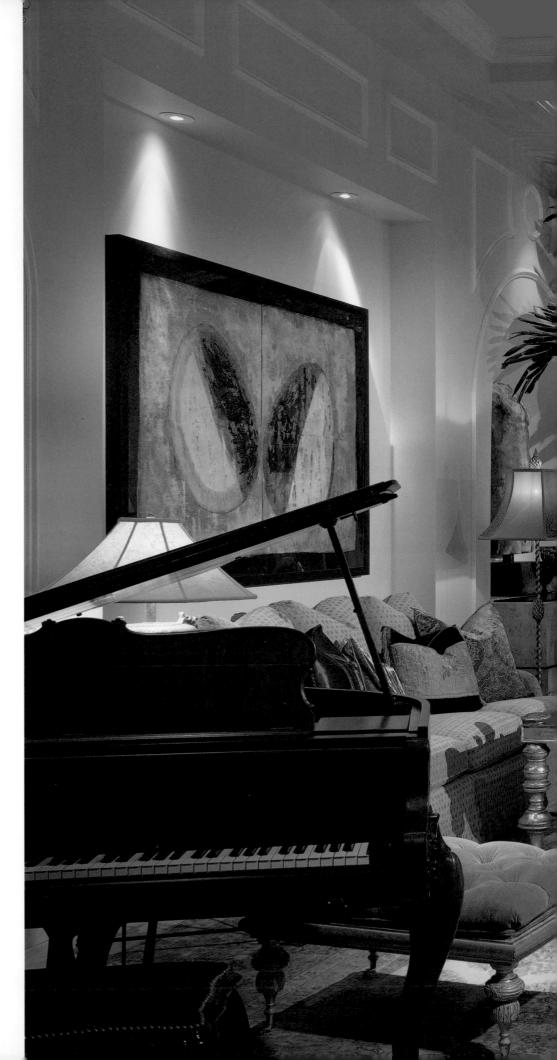

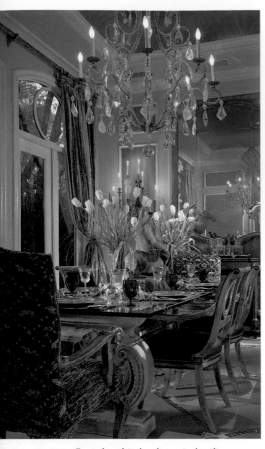

*Curved multicolored mosaic detailing
on the floor is an uexpected surprise
in this dining room—and it serves to
anchor the table.*

Location: Winter Park, Florida

[right] *With a beautiful view of the
courtyard, the opulence of this living
room is accented by the lighting.*

Location: Winter Park, Florida

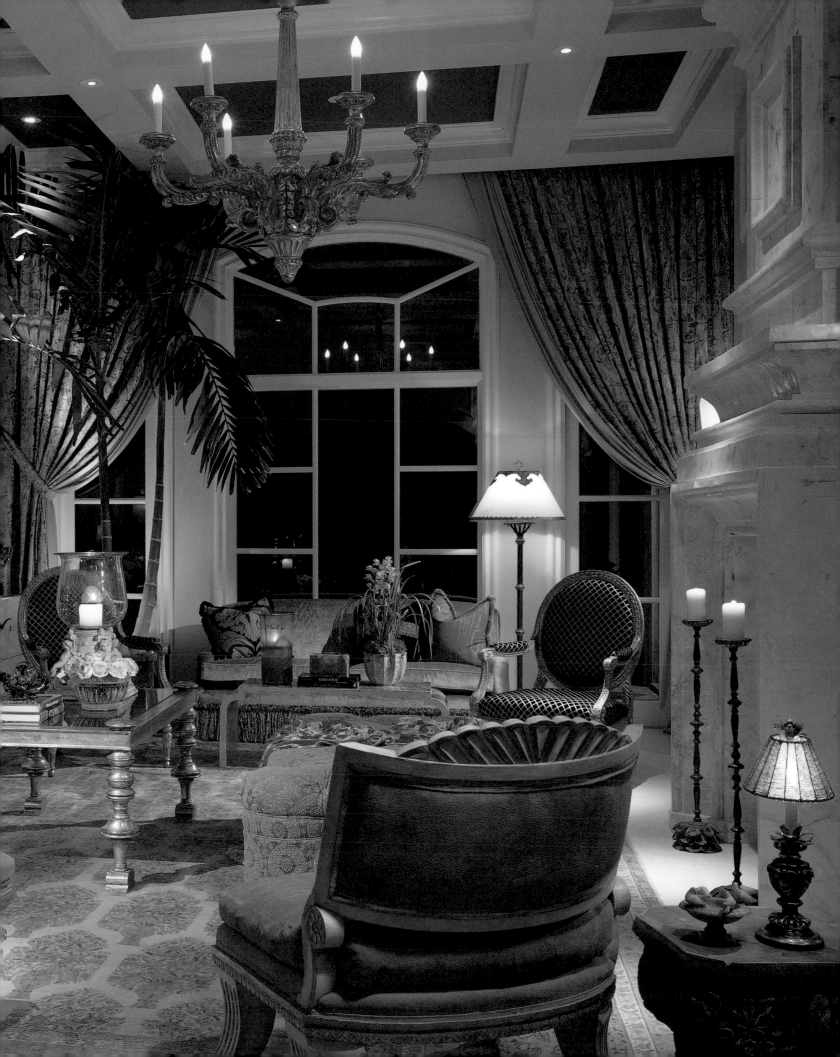

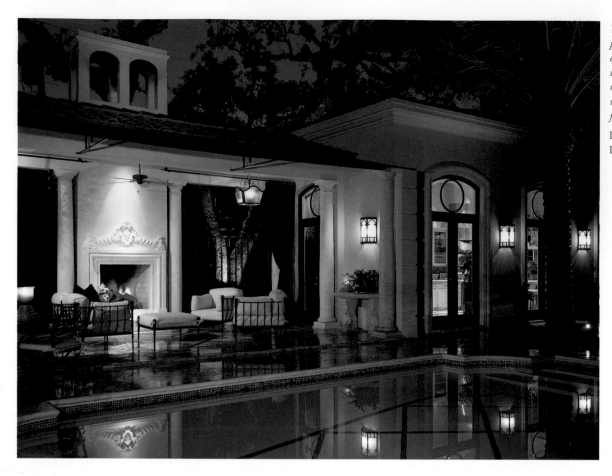

The loggia beside the pool functions as an outdoor family room—it is completely furnished and contains a wood-burning fireplace for evening enjoyment.

Location: Winter Park, Florida

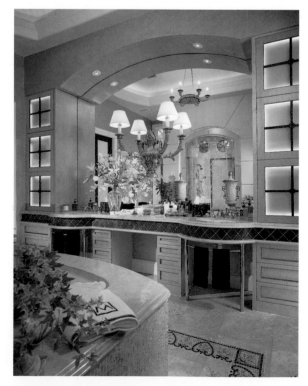

Wood, metal, stone, and tile detailing abound in the master bath.

Location: Winter Park, Florida

[right] *The kitchen has a commercial approach to design with stainless steel appliances and pot rack. The Viking range centers the room and is framed in tumbled marble and quilted steel above.*

Location: Winter Park, Florida

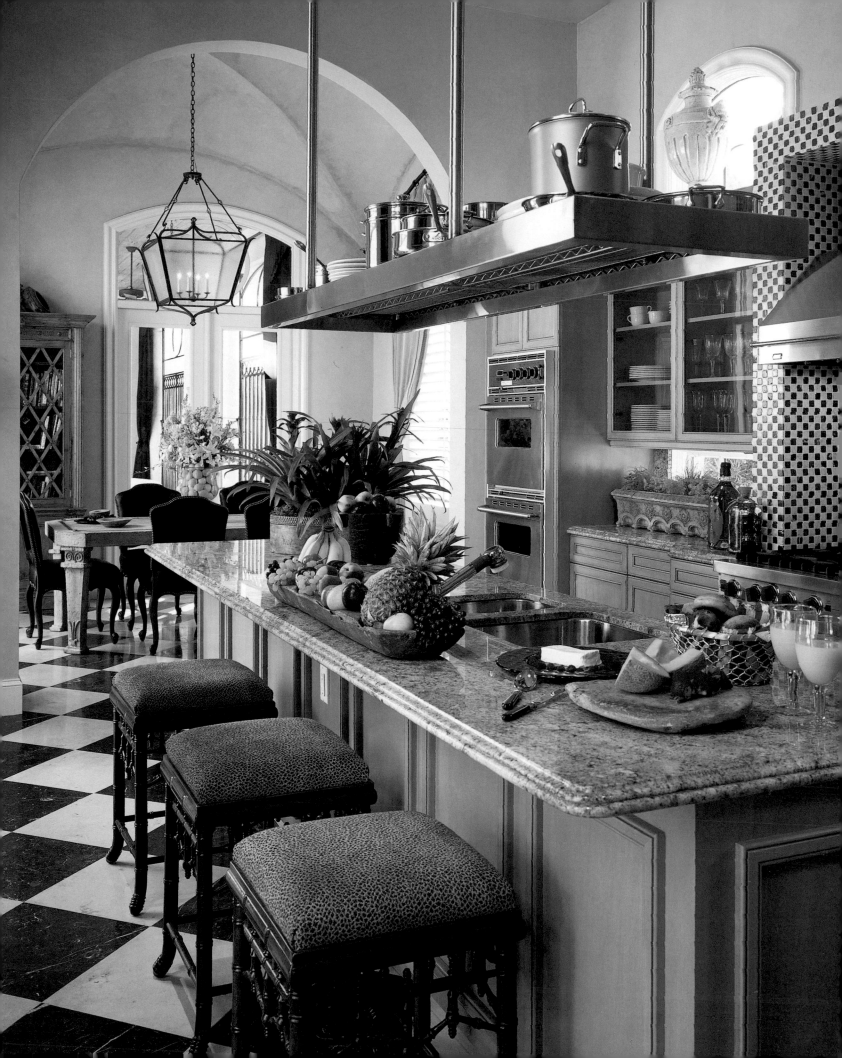

BENJAMIN NORIEGA-ORTIZ

Benjamin Noriega-Ortiz is known for his clean approach to interior design. His work is characterized by a sensible use of color and a mix of furniture styles based on shapes and textures. His taste for rich upholstery fabrics and simple materials for draperies and window treatments soften the rooms he designs while maintaining their classical air. Noriega-Ortiz is also a trained architect who designs lighting fixtures and furniture for his clients, and was recently selected by *House Beautiful* magazine as one of "Today's Stylemakers Designers" at work in America.

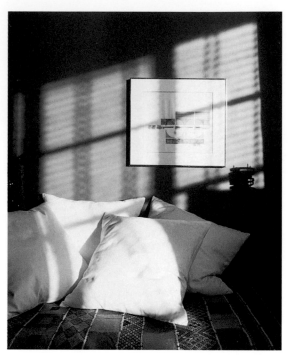

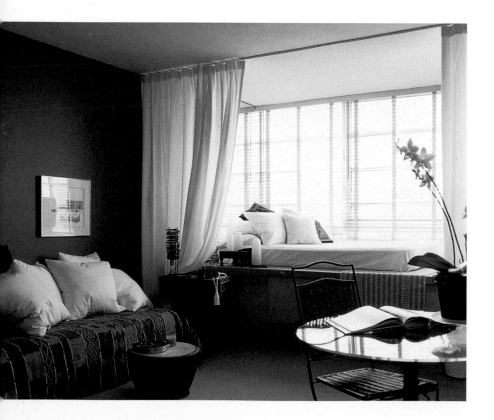

The master bedroom has been divided in two zones: sleeping chamber and sitting room. The sleeping chamber has been elevated to take advantage of the view and the sides have been mirrored to create a "bay window." Again, white is the accent against strong, richly dark hues.

Location: Miami, Florida

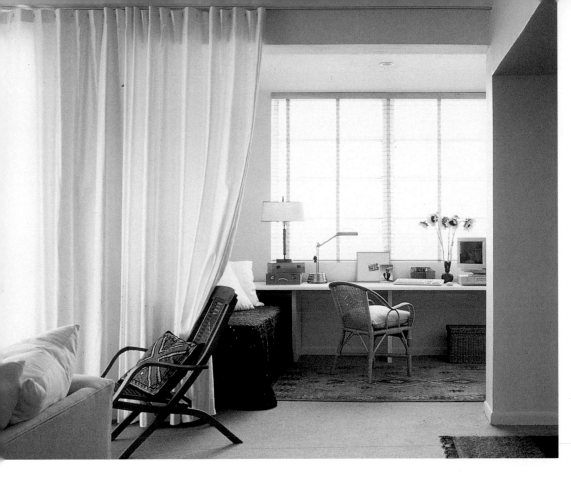

A white cotton drapery divides the living room from the study. The thin breezy fabric of the drapery reflects light and becomes a large scale "lantern."

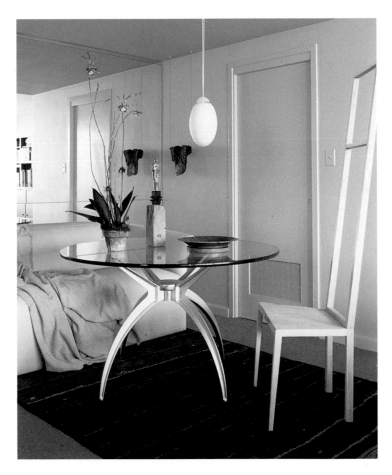

[right] *The mirrored dining alcove reflects the view of the water on the opposite wall. The aqua on the walls is extended to include the ceiling in this lower area of the apartment.*

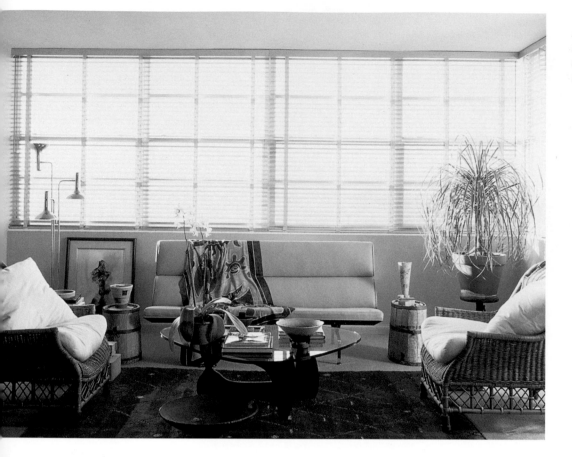

The International Style pieces such as the Eames sofa and the Noguchi coffee table interact perfectly with a vintage Moroccan carpet. Two inch thick wood jealousy blinds complete the tropical look

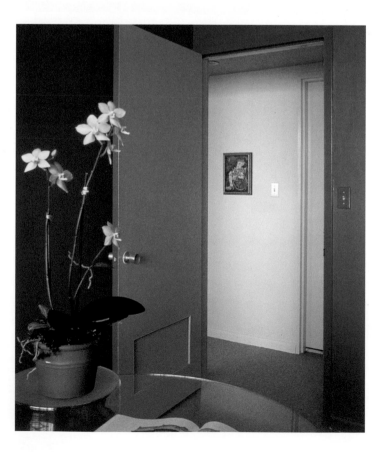

At the end of the hallway, all the colors of the apartment converge, summarizing the color concept of the design.

Location: Miami, Florida

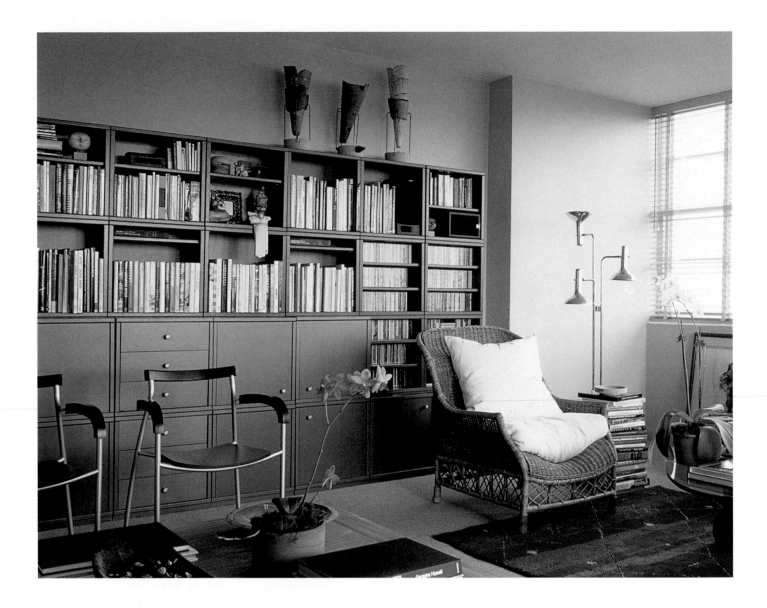

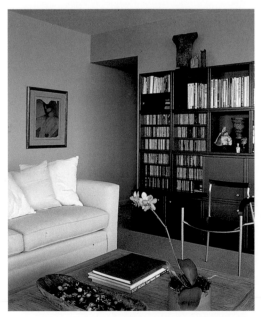

The interior resembles interiors from the 1940s in Miami Beach. The use of the modular Danish bookcase contributes to the warmth of the room.

PEDLAR'S VILLAGE INTERIOR DESIGN

As an interior designer, Gary Ficht's goal is to understand a client's lifestyle and personal tastes through conversation and observation and then translate that philosophy into a classic design that will be aesthetically pleasing, functional, and enduring. A sense of comfort and a spirit of vitality are key.

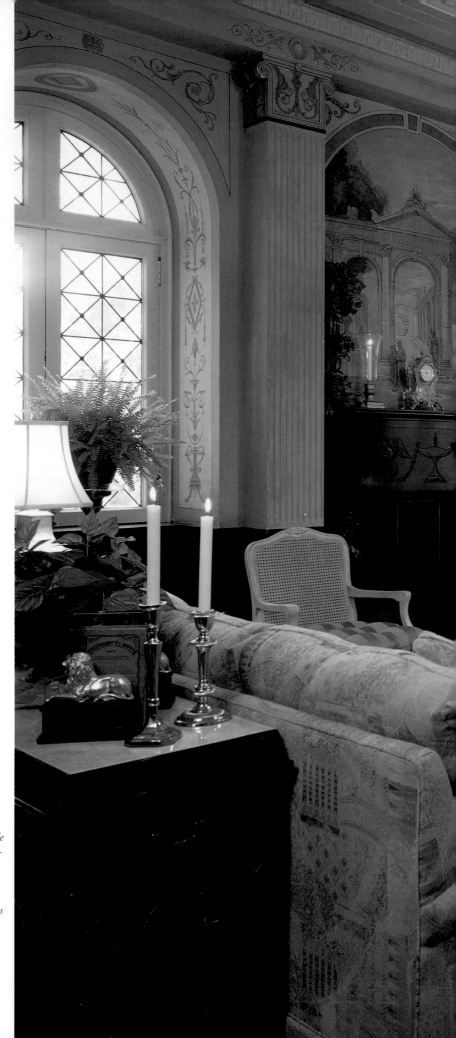

The elegance of classic traditional style instills this room with a sense of time-lessness. The rug and the bordered marble floor echo the ornate painted ceiling. A mix of wood finishes, glass and brass accents, and Fortuny fabrics enhance the room's architectural character.

Location: Sarasota, Florida

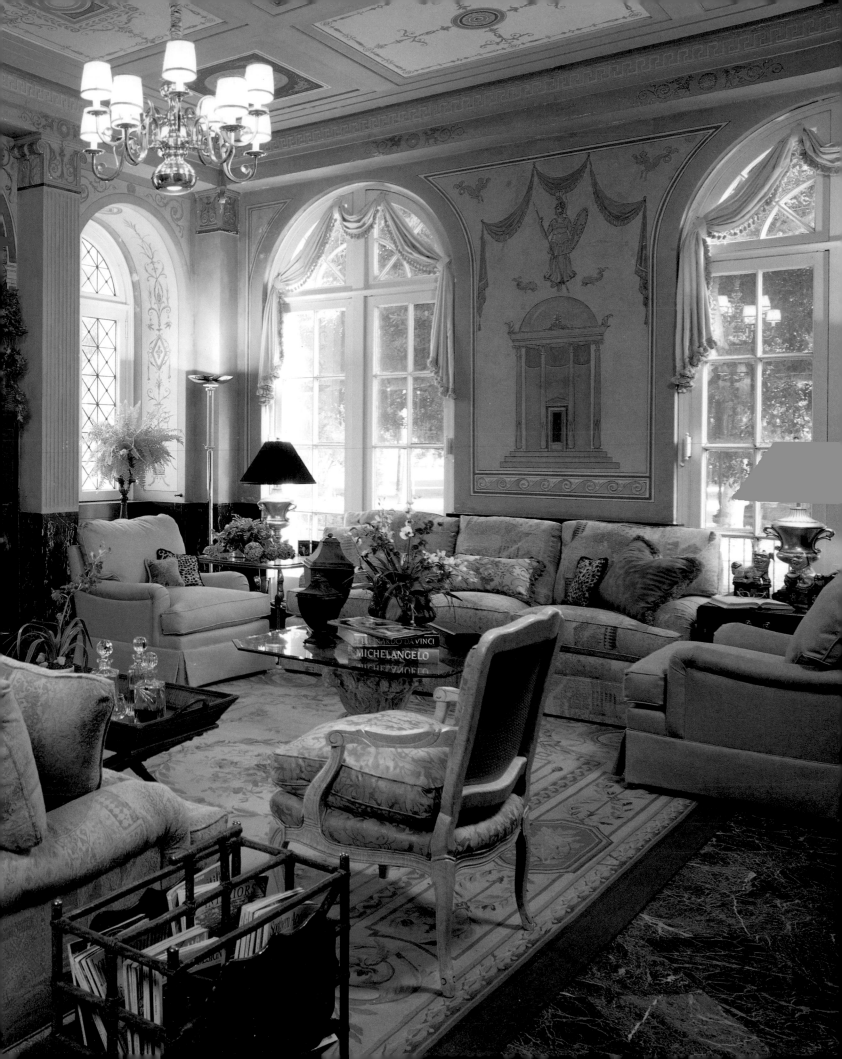

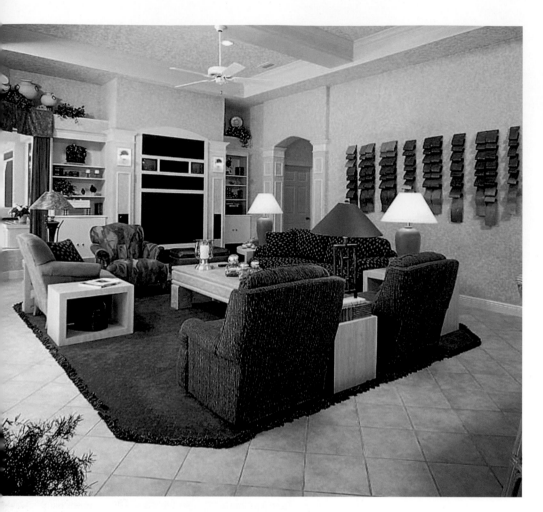

Textures, motion, and color come together in this visually stimulating media room. The colors of an abstract wall sculpture are repeated in the upholstery on the pair of comfortable chairs. The room's sleek surfaces and furniture are countered with a nubby fabric for the sofa and other chairs.

Location: Sarasota, Florida

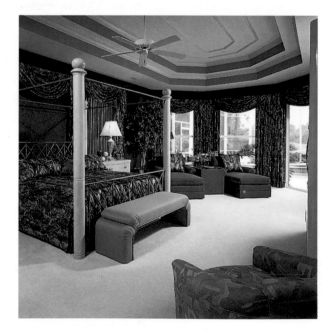

Aubergine walls enlivened with an elegant faux finish, bold gemstone colored fabrics, and warm touches of gold accents instill excitement in this master bedroom.

Location: Sarasota, Florida

Tall ceilings and faux-finished walls create a dramatic dining experience. Sculptured carpet and a mirror over the marble-topped, built-in buffet enhance the room's striking scheme.

Location: Sarasota, Florida

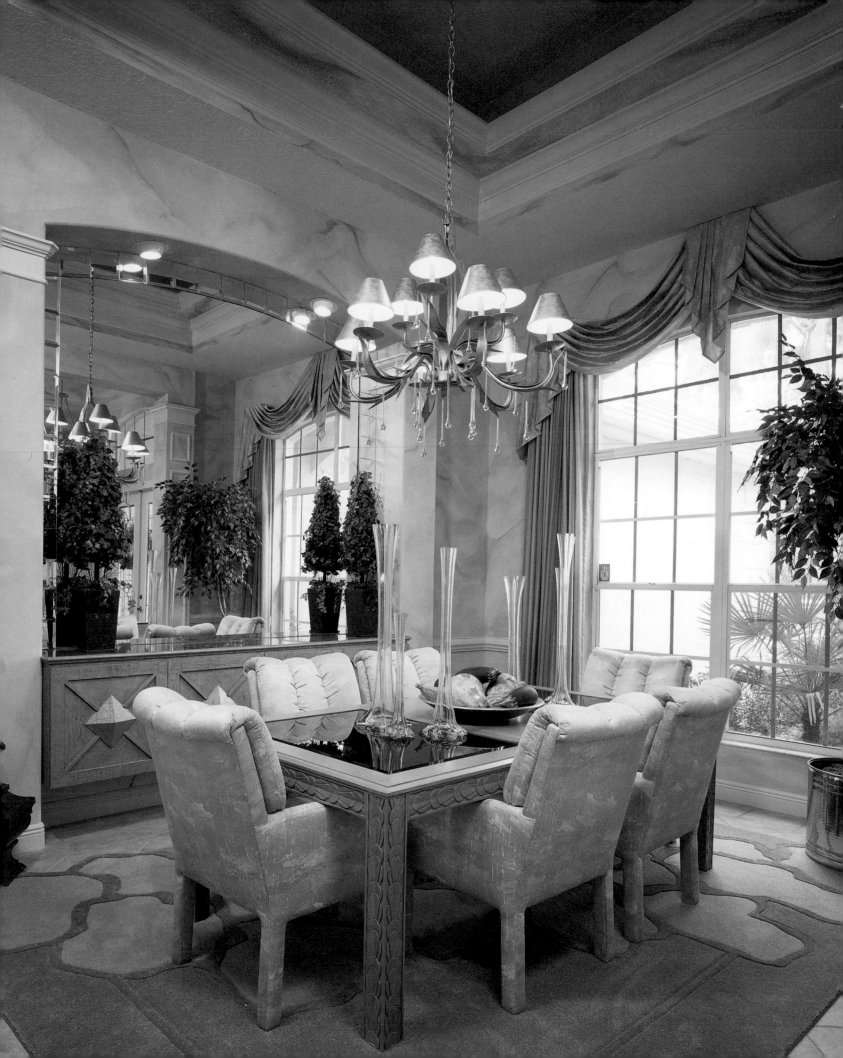

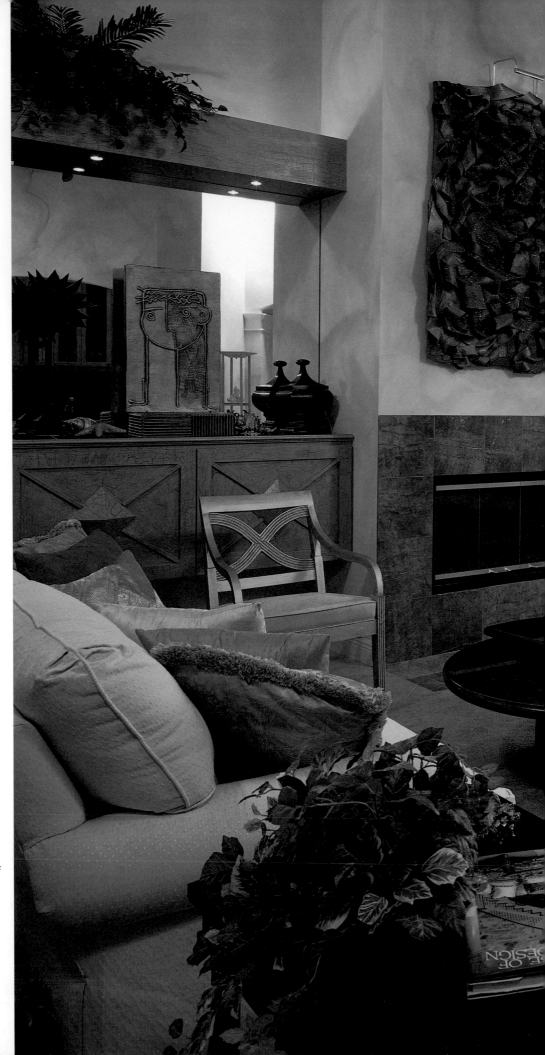

A simple, yet elegant window treatment of silver/gray Fortuny damask combined with tones of mauve and tangerine takes advantage of the room's vistas to the great outdoors.

Location: Sarasota, Florida

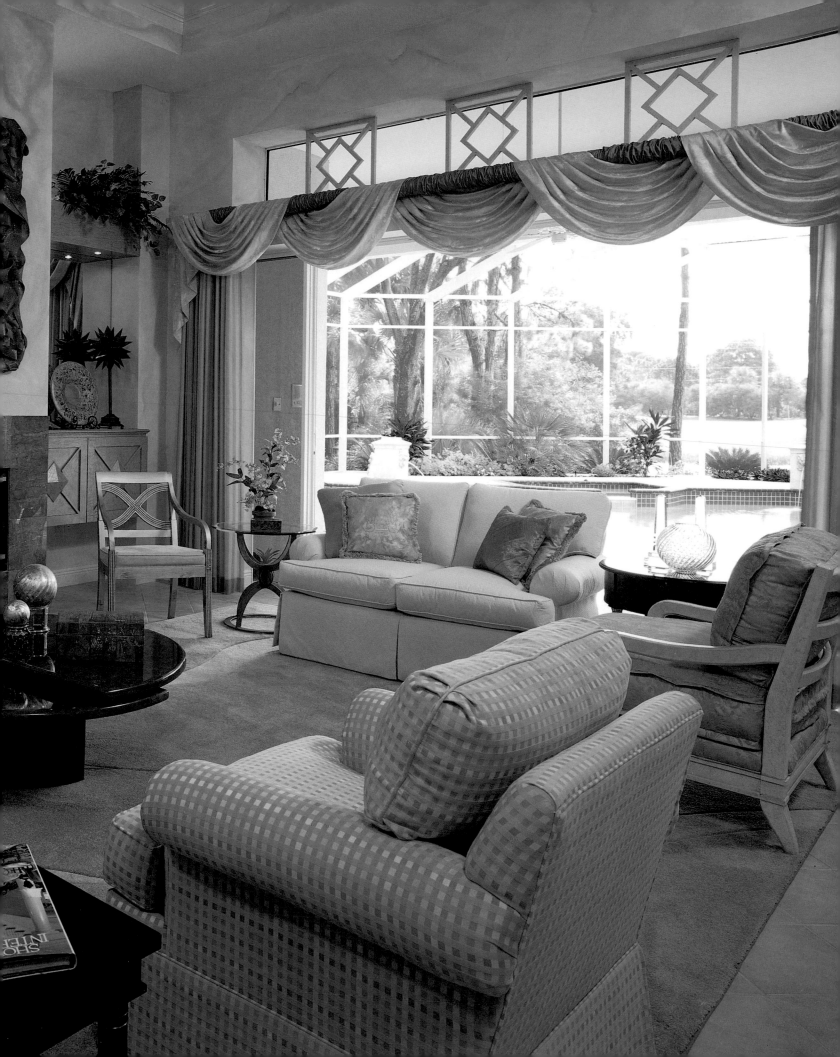

PIANO NOBILE

A space should be aesthetically pleasing and visually engaging, as well as highly functional. Light, color, and proportion are key. Personal touches above and beyond the furniture, fabrics, and accessories give the room its unique character and make it complete.

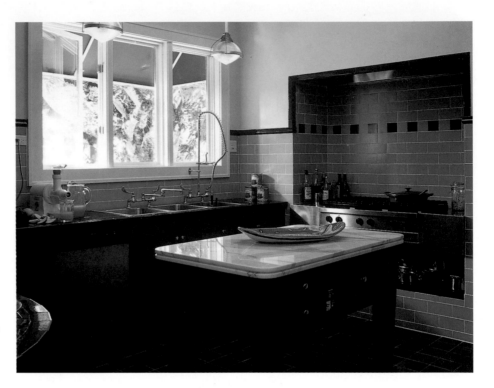

This modern interpretation of a country kitchen consists of a green-tiled wall five-feet high combined with frame and panel-inset wooden cabinets. Light fixtures over the sink enhance the kitchen's industrial feel.

Location: Coral Gables, Florida

[right] *A tall, arched window floods this urbane breakfast nook with natural light. The designer's own custom table pairs a base inspired by the Art Nouveau designs of Victor Horta of Paris with a terrazzo top.*

Location: Coral Gables, Florida

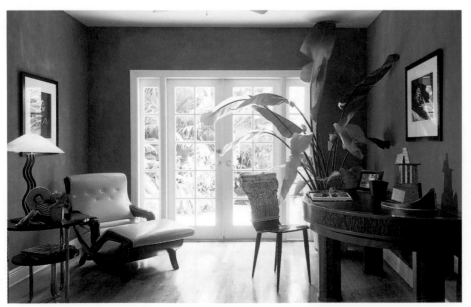

In keeping with the tropical Modern theme, clean-line Art Deco blends with Miami Sorbet colors to create a cool refreshing interior that rests the eye and leaves the Miami heat outdoors. The royal palm desk was crafted from recycled wood salvaged after hurricane Andrew. The Art Deco chaise and Gilbert Rhode table date from the 1930s.

Location: Coconut Grove, Florida

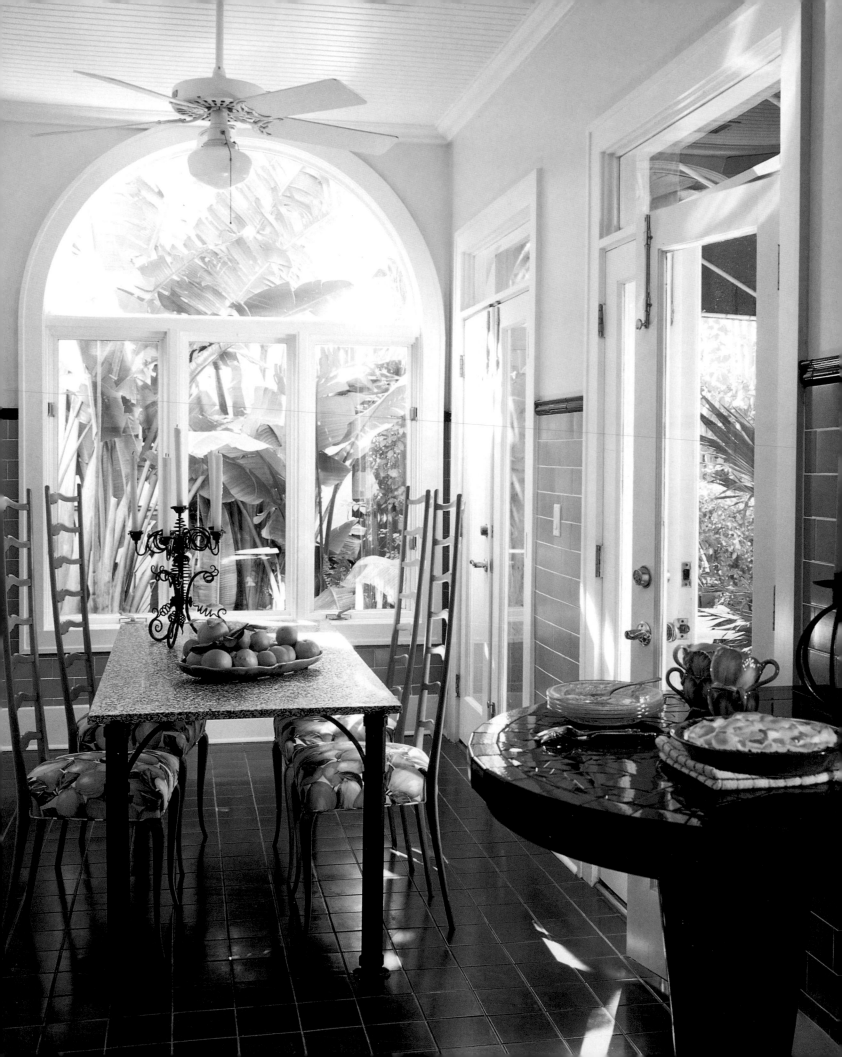

RETRO INTERIORS, INC.

Retro Interiors is best known for its unusually artistic approach to interior design. Primarily traditional in nature, Retro Interiors gives each project a special flavor that represents the individual client's personality. Traditional designs and classical elements are enhanced by drawing from eclectic influences including ethnic, domestic, and contemporary references. Retro Interiors also exerts a strong hand in the use of color, texture, and accessories. The firm, consisting of a team of eight designers, assistants, and draftsmen, strives to create interiors that are aesthically pleasing and make people feel at home immediately.

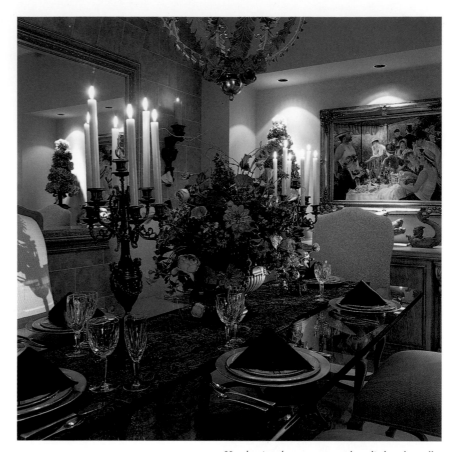

Hand-painted canvas, cut and applied to the wall in the pattern of concrete blocks, adds weight as a backdrop for a luxurious dining area. The built-in buffet incorporates hand-carved corbels brought back from Honduras by the designer.

Location: Lighthouse Point, Florida

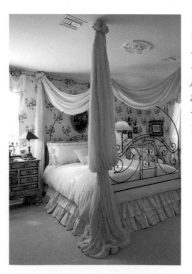

Created as a retreat for the owner's wife to read and reminisce, this room is filled with charm and grace. The iron bed was draped in gauze and fabrics appears layered like a wedding gown. Authentic accents and accessories date back to the early 1800s.

Location: Lighthouse Point, Florida

[right] Faux books add illusion to an otherwise difficult wall. The seating is a leather frame sectional with upholstered cushions in chenille fabric. Dark draperies add a warming effect to a side window.

Location: Lighthouse Point, Florida

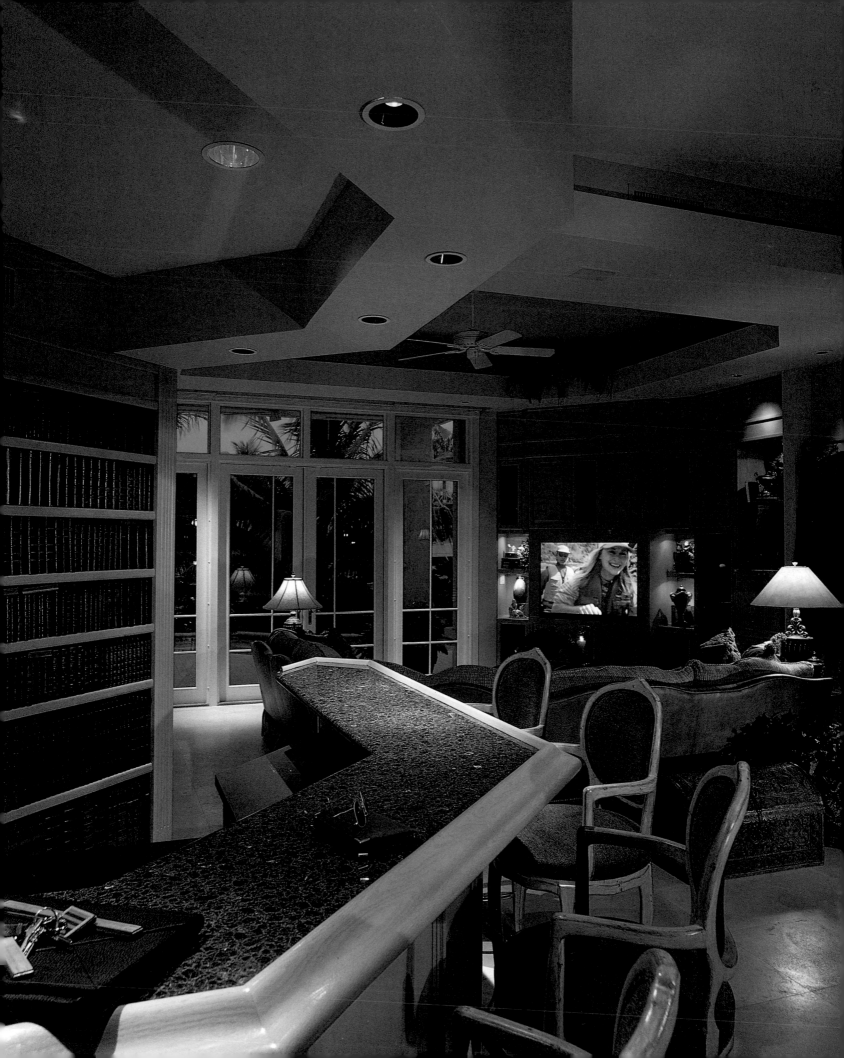

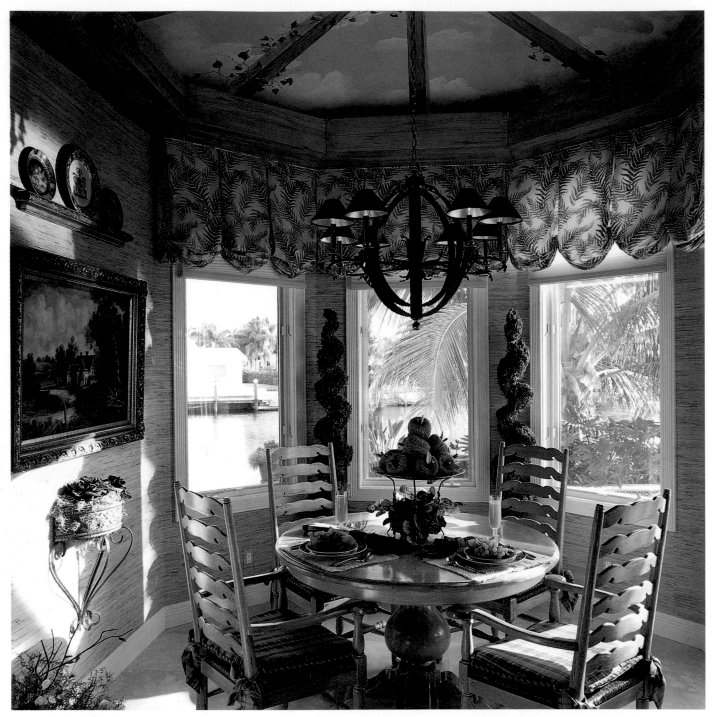

A faux soffit and gazebo mural give this breakfast area a special identity. Textured walls, stone flooring, distressed furnishings, topiaries, and lots of natural sunlight make this a perfect area to start the day.

Location: Lighthouse Point, Florida

[right] A grand family room captures the flavor of this showhome. Designed to represent the home of extensive collectors and travelers, lavish accessories were creatively placed, including use of drapery finials on tribal spears.

Location: Fort Lauderdale, Florida

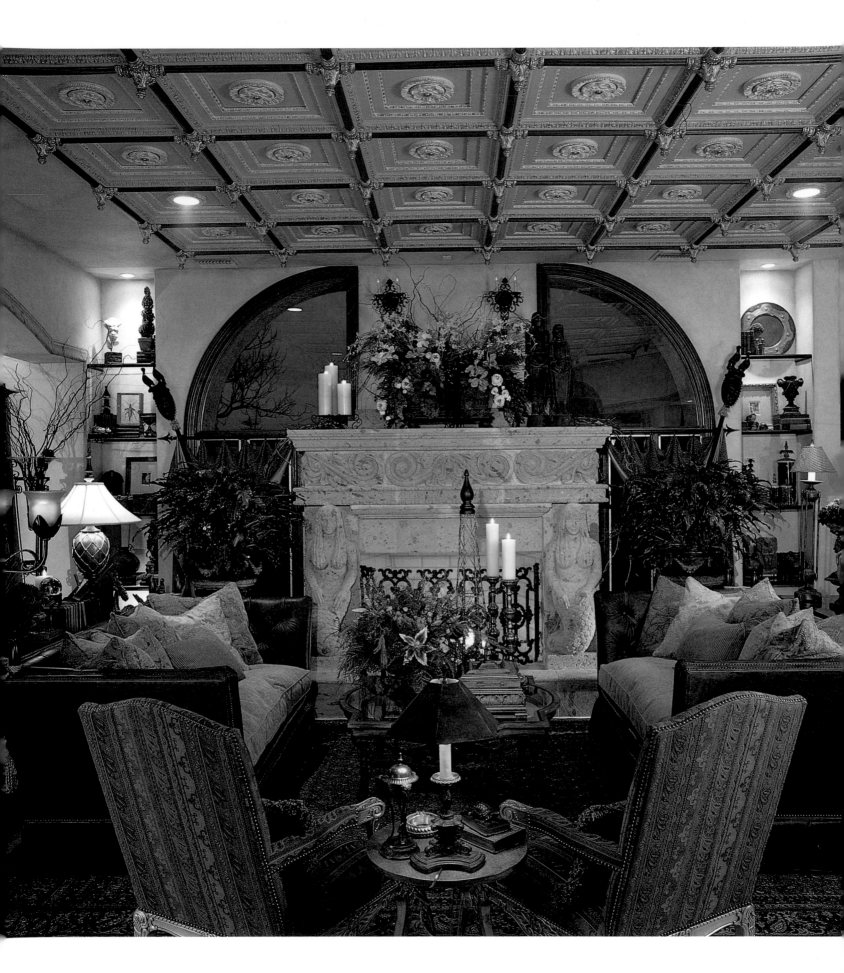

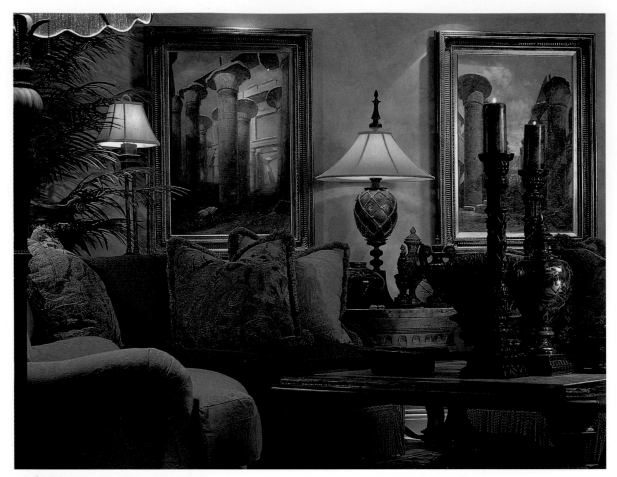

Richly colored fabrics and finely selected furnishings add depth and interest to a small living room, creating an intimate yet dramatic interior. Scale and placement play a skillful part to make this room beautiful to the eye yet wonderful to live in.

Location: Lighthouse Point, Florida

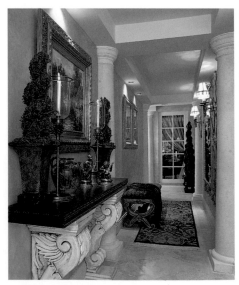

An otherwise bland hallway was transformed by lifting the ceiling and adding lit soffits with stone columns to break up the space. The stationary door at the end of the hall adds intrigue and creates a side entrance to the living room.

Location: Fort Lauderdale, Florida

[right] *Individually upholstered squares applied to the headboard wall imbue this bedroom with a sense of elegance. An iron gate was transformed into the headboard. Lighting was designed to highlight the texture of the wall while keeping the rest of the room dark and romantic.*

Location: Lighthouse Point, Florida

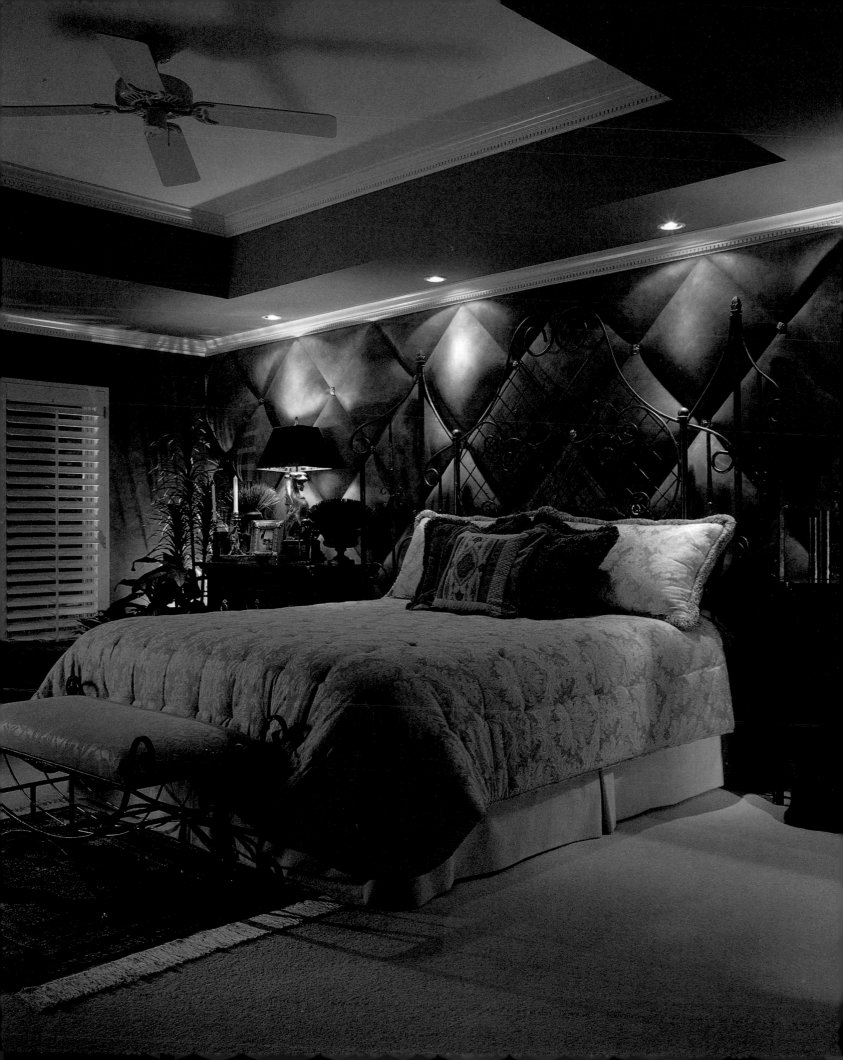

ROD MICKLEY INTERIOR DESIGN

Rod Mickley prides himself in his ability to interpret his clients' taste, vision, and lifestyle, and translate them into an appealing and functional reality. With this in mind, each design is a unique statement respecting the homeowner, as well as the architectural integrity of the residence. Attention to scale, color, detail, and function is an integral component of his designs.

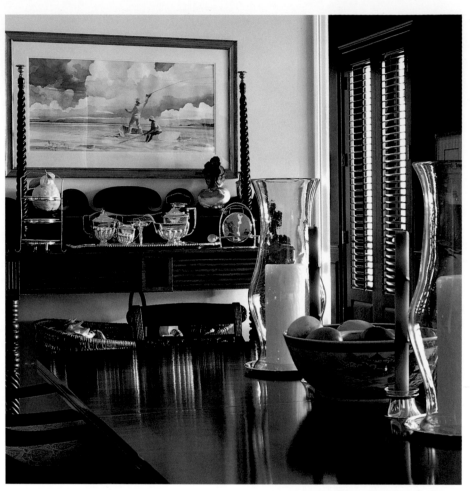

A tall, antique sideboard provides a distinctive focal point and reflects the decidedly Caribbean feel of this engaging dining area. A mix of accessories and a large watercolor complements the dark woods of the furnishings and architectural details.

Location: Vero Beach, Florida

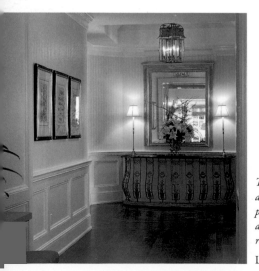

The foyer, with its natural palette and refined architectural detailing, presents an elegant first impression and functions as a hub to all the rooms of the house.

Location: Vero Beach, Florida

[right] *This elegant and inviting living room doesn't hold an allegiance to any style but offers an eclectic approach that reflects the best of all worlds.*

Location: Vero Beach, Florida

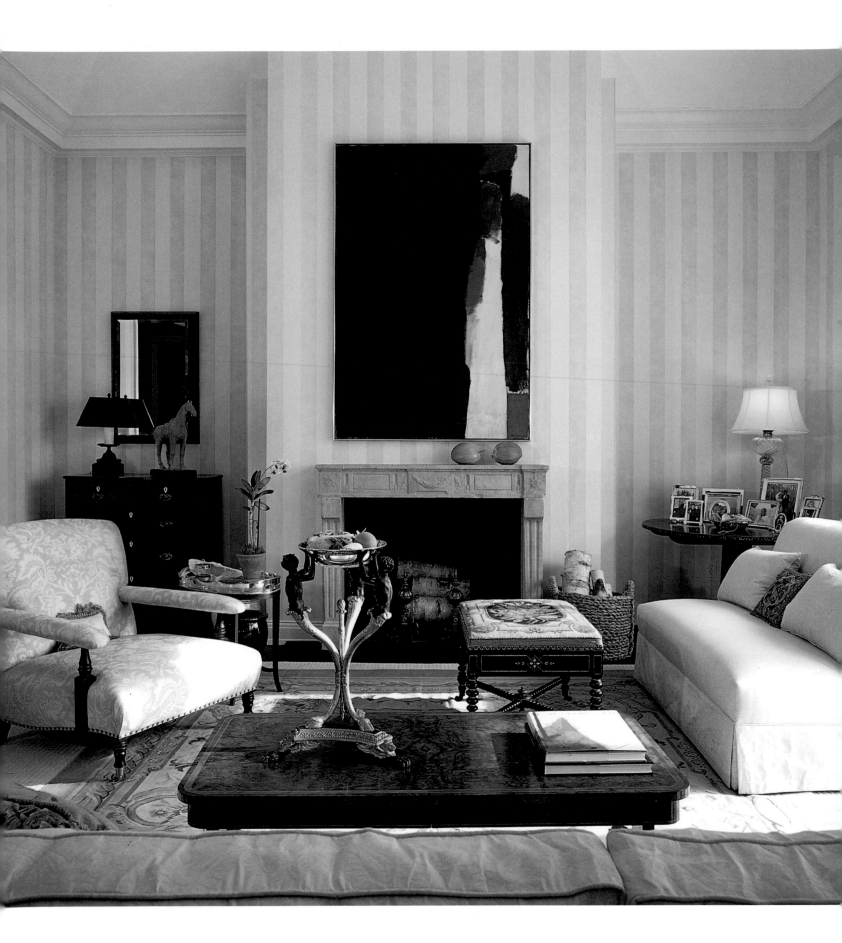

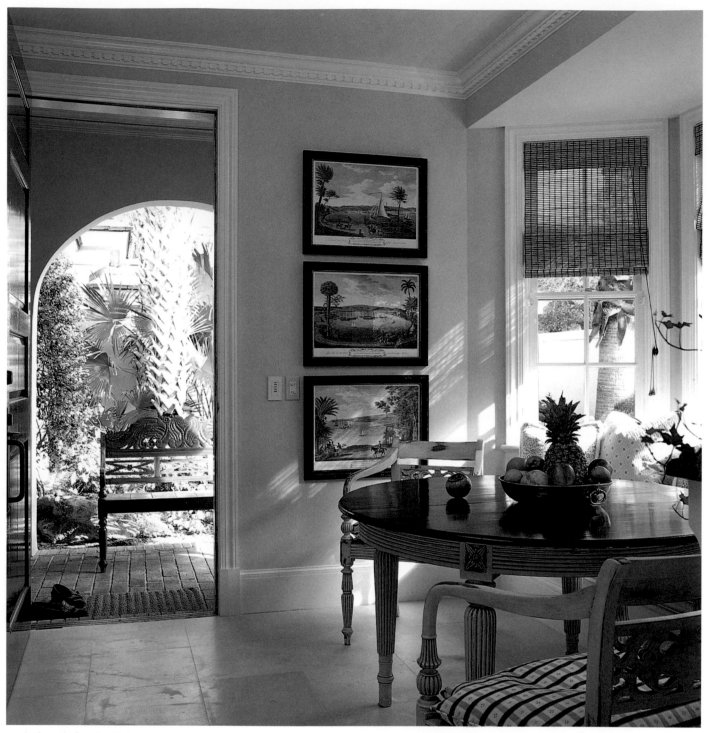

At the far end of a galley kitchen, a window seat acts as part of the breakfast room seating. The table base and chairs are painted distressed white to give the room a more tropical-island feel.

Location: Vero Beach, Florida

[right] *Blue and white sets the theme for this grand, yet comfortable, family room overlooking the St. John's River.*

Location: Vero Beach, Florida

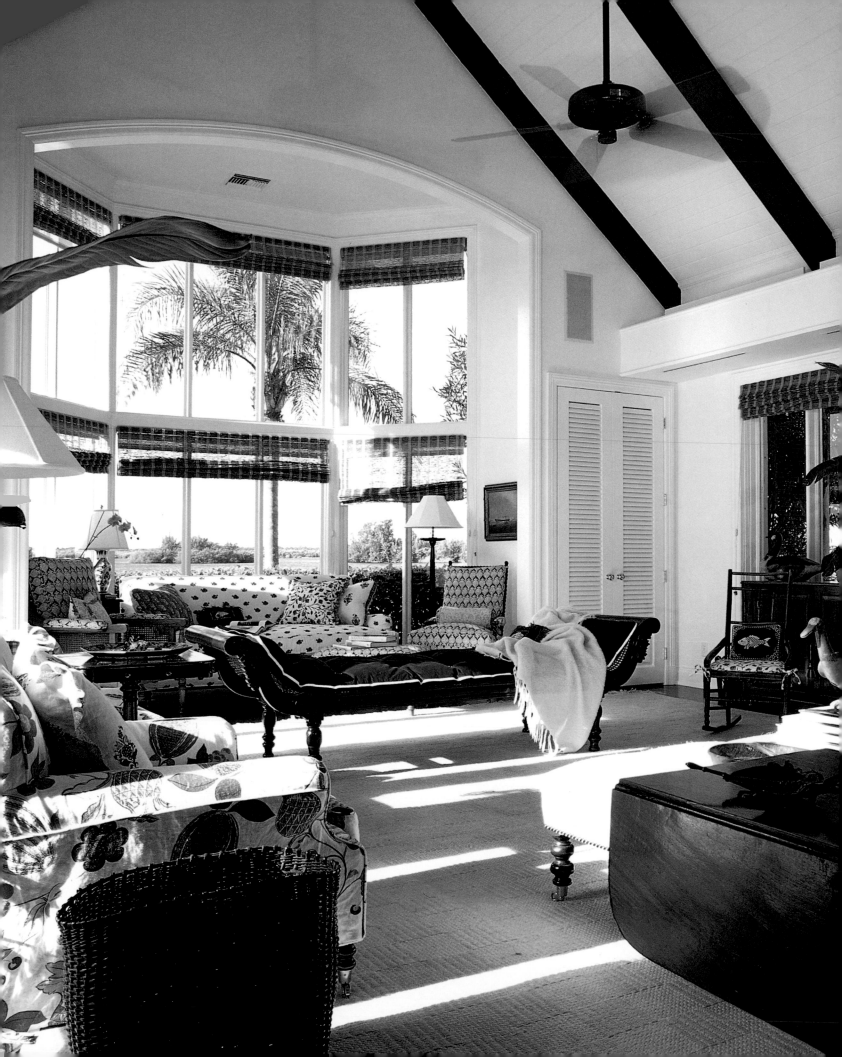

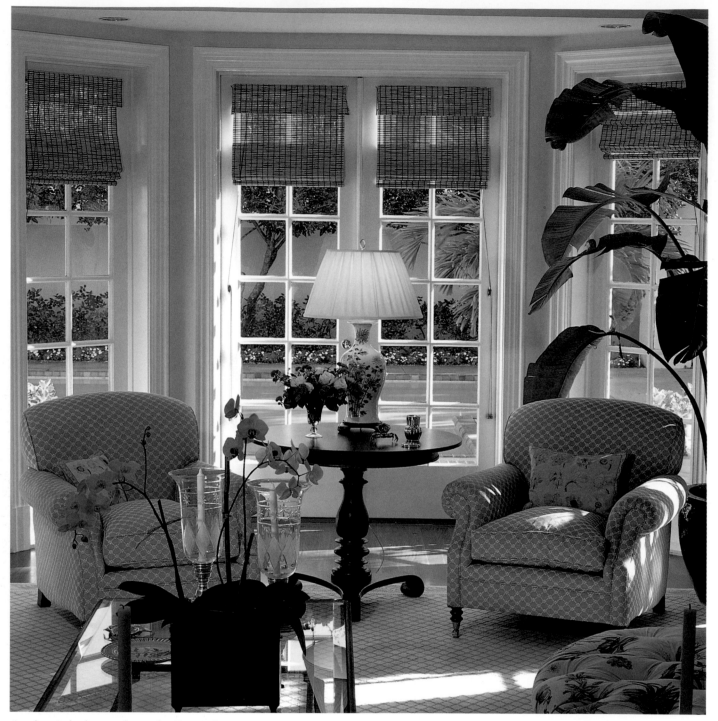

A cool tropical palette sets the tone for this coastal residence. Wainscot walls, paneled openings, and tall doors add architectural interest.

Location: Vero Beach, Florida

In the dining room, a niche was created to allow the table to be set on an angle to take advantage of natural light from the adjacent living room and lanai.

Location: Vero Beach, Florida

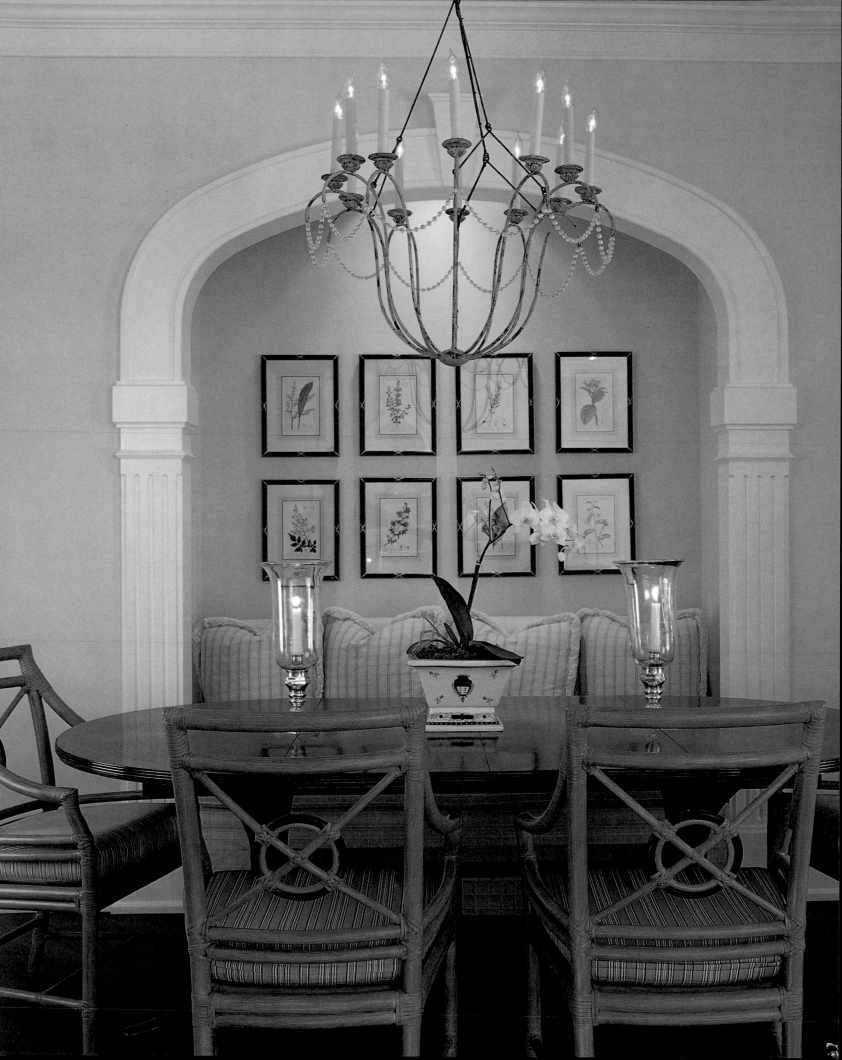

SPECTRUM INTERIOR DESIGN

Spectrum's team takes a fresh, innovative approach to interior design. The firm believes that space is an extension of individual lifestyle. Their strength lies in the ability to blend color and architecture into a place of understated elegance and charm. Just as a conductor leads his orchestra through the intricacies of a symphony, these designers gently guide each of the clients through the design process. The result is a space filled with harmony and balance, yet orchestrated down to the smallest detail. Spectrum's design philosophy is simply to combine the finest fabrics and furnishings with unusual textures and finishes, translating these materials into a distinctive, timeless environment.

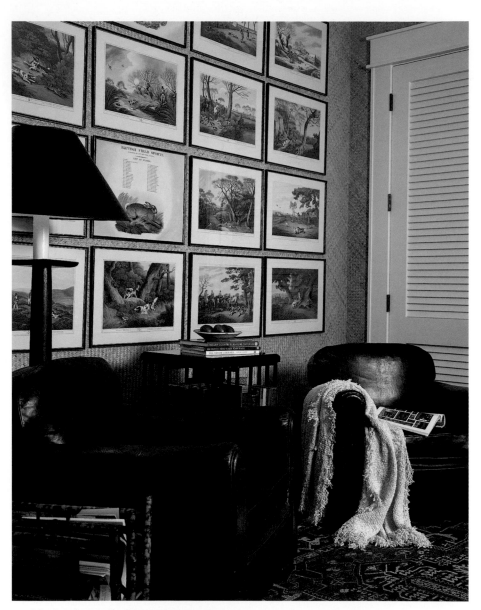

Dark leather chairs and an Oriental rug, accented by a collection of British hunting scenes arranged against a neutral, textured wallcovering make for an engaging, masculine retreat.

Location: Vero Beach, Florida

Traditional furnishings and a striking accent fabric lend formality to this dining area, while the golden hues of the walls and an abundance of natural light instill drama in the space.

Location: Vero Beach, Florida

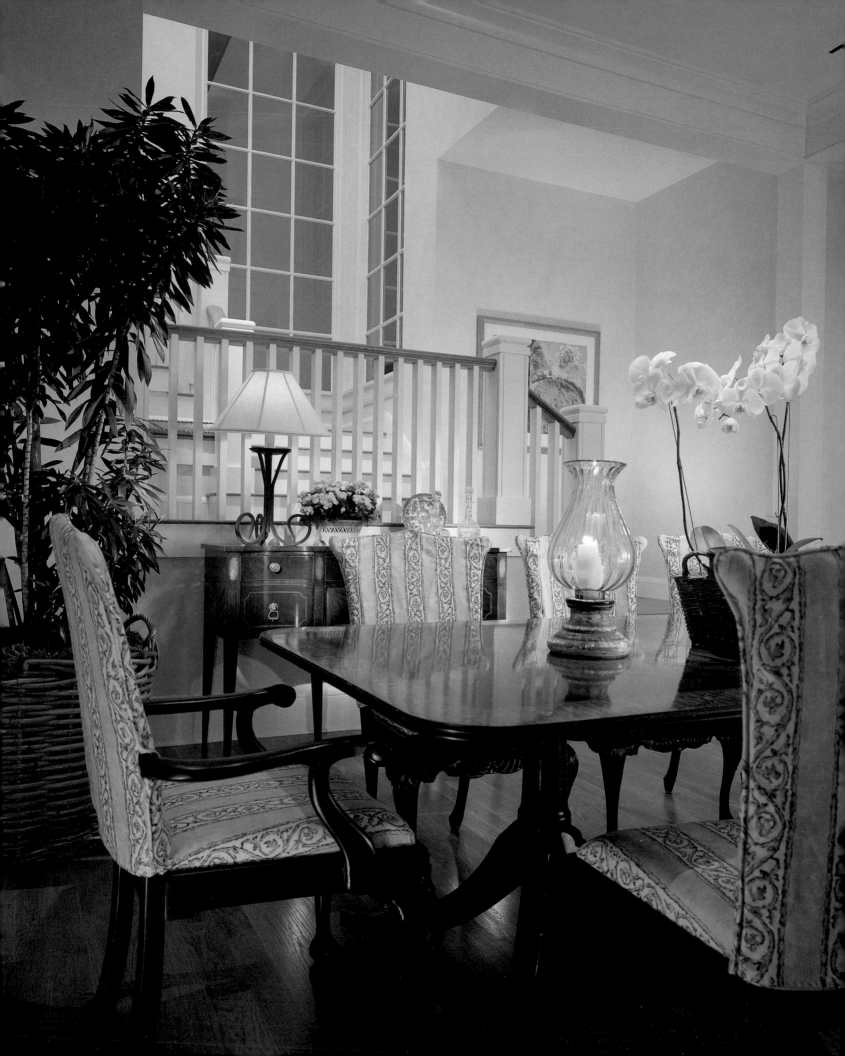

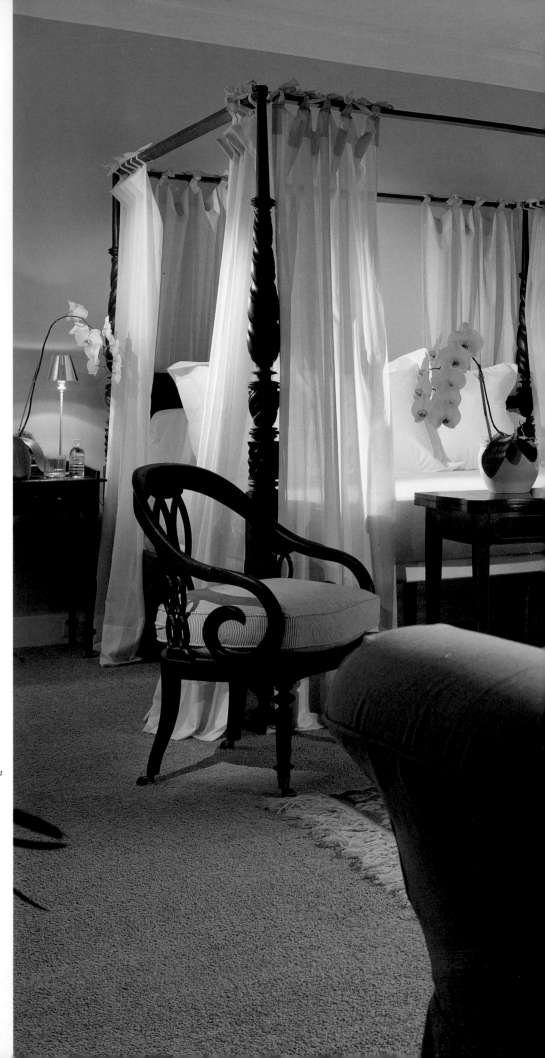

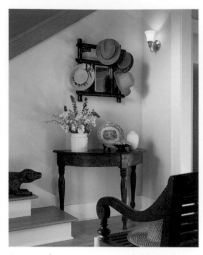

Deep mahogany contrasts with bleached wood floors at a new home in the renowned community of Windsor, Florida. A selection of jaunty straw hats completes the mood for the entrance to this delightful retreat.

Location: Vero Beach, Florida

This master suite takes advantage of ocean breezes with its French doors and plantation bed softly draped with fabric. Colors and furnishings reflect the tropical splendor of the traditional British colonial architecture.

Location: Vero Beach, Florida

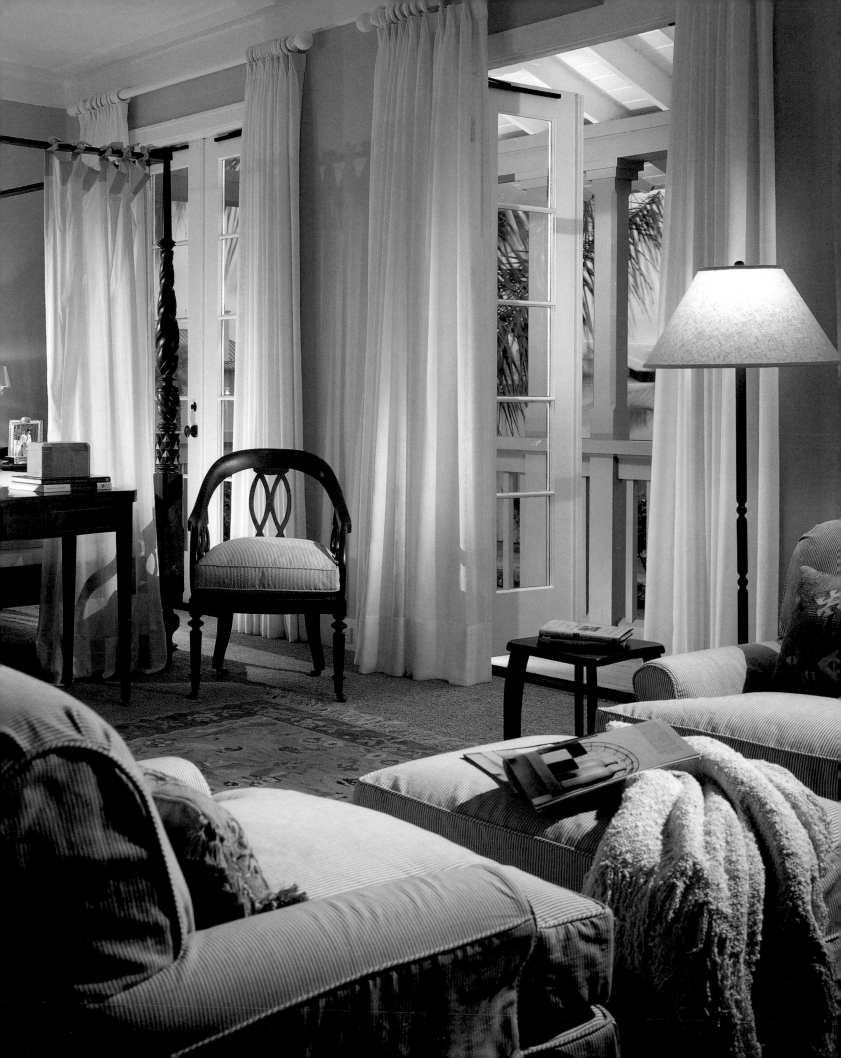

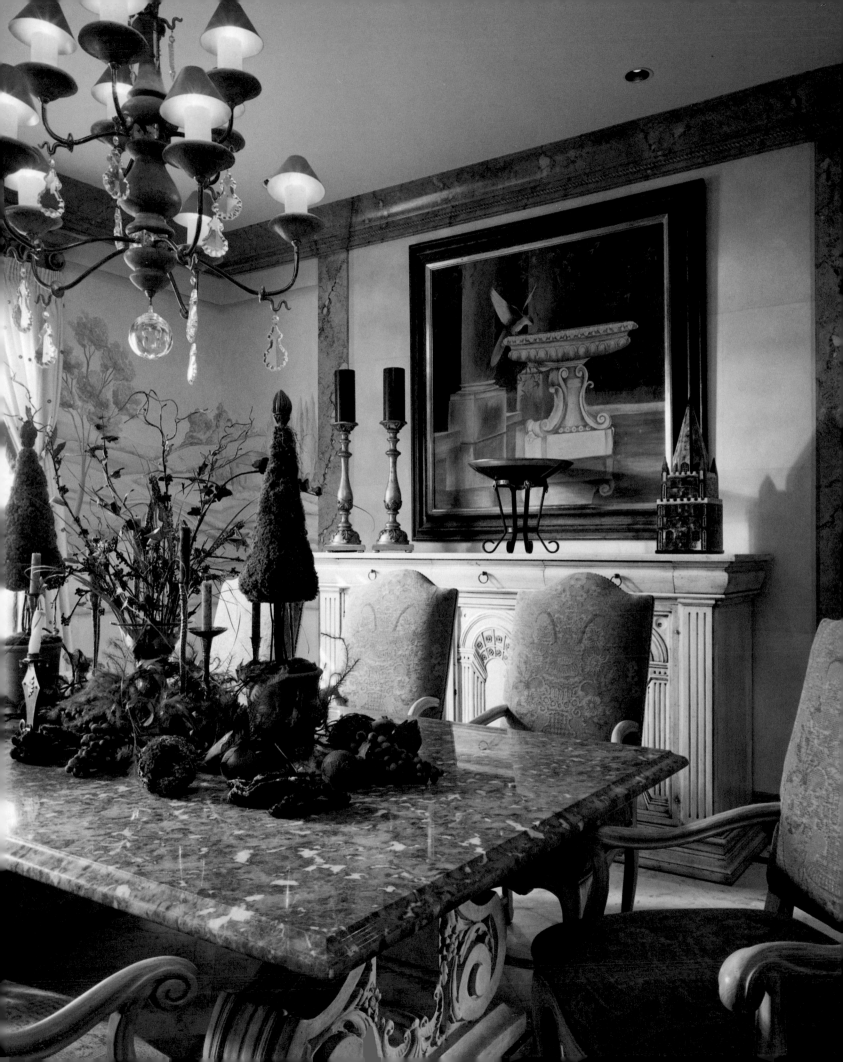

DEEP
SOUTH

By most estimations—whether they are fired by romantic notions or strict geographical demarcations—this is the real South. "The rich magnolias covered with fragrant blossoms, the holly, the beech, the tall yellow poplar, the hilly ground and even the red clay, all excited my admiration," wrote artist and naturalist John James Audubon in his journal on his arrival at Oakley Plantation in St. Francisville, Louisiana, in 1821. Even today, in the plantation country of Louisiana, gray-green Spanish moss drifts in chiffon-like streamers from live oak trees and the stately antebellum houses look much the same as they did in the nineteenth century.

The South's "deepness" is a suggestion not only of the mystery of the lush and verdant states of Georgia, Alabama, Mississippi, the Carolinas, Louisiana, and Virginia, but also a reminder of the separation these states have maintained from the rest of the country. There are reasons why the South is a place apart: as a region is has always been more in tune with Old World culture than with the clamor and industry of the rest of the United States.

[left] *A marble-top Italian table combined with tapestry chairs and a hand-painted mural create a theatrical dining experience. Tall ceilings and ornate architectural detailing magnify the room's sense of drama.*

Interior Design: Leo Dowell Interiors, Inc.
Location: Hamptonville, North Carolina

Its allegiance with Great Britain and France is historical—in 1682 Rene Robert Cavelier, sieur de la Salle reached the mouth of the Mississippi River, took formal possession of the land it drains, and named the vast area Louisiana after his king Louis XIV. For a century the land remained distinctly French, and the philosophical vestiges linger into the late twentieth century. France, the great individualist among nations, exudes energetic pride doing things stylishly and with zest. In the south today, piquant and complex etouffees, fried oysters with cajun tartar sauce, catfish beignets, and creole mustard soup are savory reminders of a not-too-distant heritage. Houses—small chateaus and homey Creole cottages both old and new—keep the French heritage alive. A new cultural element was introduced to the mix in 1763 when France ceded to Great Britain all territory east of the Mississippi except New Orleans.

British settlers began to populate the area—especially Virginia, where planters built spectacular Georgian mansions along the rivers of the Tidewater. Awe-inspiring and opulent, they testified to the great planters' wealth and prominence. As intellectual statements they were symbols that the state's leaders were abreast of the latest European ideas. The self-confident Virginia gentry liked to think of their estates as retreats from the world of

commerce, and since there were few roads and towns, most colonists made their homes their own little worlds. Formality and correctness were just another way of making private worlds special.

It is not much different today, although most houses are smaller and the outside world is more inescapable. The interior designers whose work is represented in these pages have created worlds of their own for their clients. Life in the south still revolves around gracious living and pride in "Southern-ness." Manners are important, and entertaining is part of good manners. You will see here wonderful spaces for gathering with friends: dining rooms that suit for both lavish parties and intimate family meals; luxurious living rooms that provide a peaceful setting for conversation; romantic bedrooms that offer sybaritic respite from a harried day. And the southern heritage—both French and English—is still thriving—not as a dim relic of a long-gone past, but in new and up-to-the minute interpretations that still make sense in a hectic modern world.

ANN CARTER INC.

Defining a design philosophy isn't easy. Ann Carter aims for a style that is timeless, allowing gracious interiors to evolve and designing rooms that grow more beautiful with the passing years. Great pleasure is derived by working with each individual client for a personal look, whether it is a mannered period scheme, a seaside summer house or a casual family home in the Southern vernacular. Clients should invest in classic items that they will treasure through the years. The best designer/client relationships develop over time, acquiring a finished look slowly and carefully. A melange of lovely things, whether antique or new, recently acquired or handed down through generations, is a look the firm strives to help others achieve. Each interior becomes an eclectic blend that is uniquely traditional, with a twist.

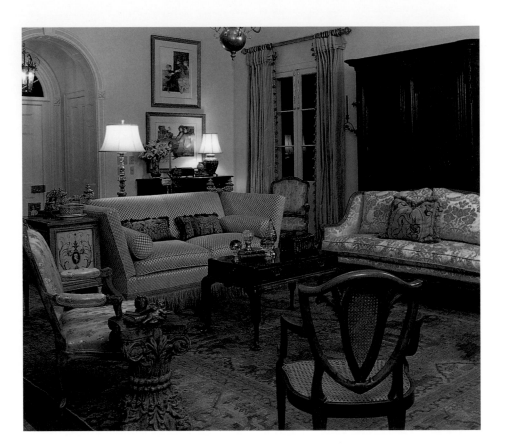

[top and right] *Elegance and comfort dwell harmoniously in this formal sitting room. French and English antiques, contemporary artwork, and rich fabrics in mellow tints provide a quiet backdrop for the owner's collection of beautiful accessories.*

Location: Jackson, Mississippi

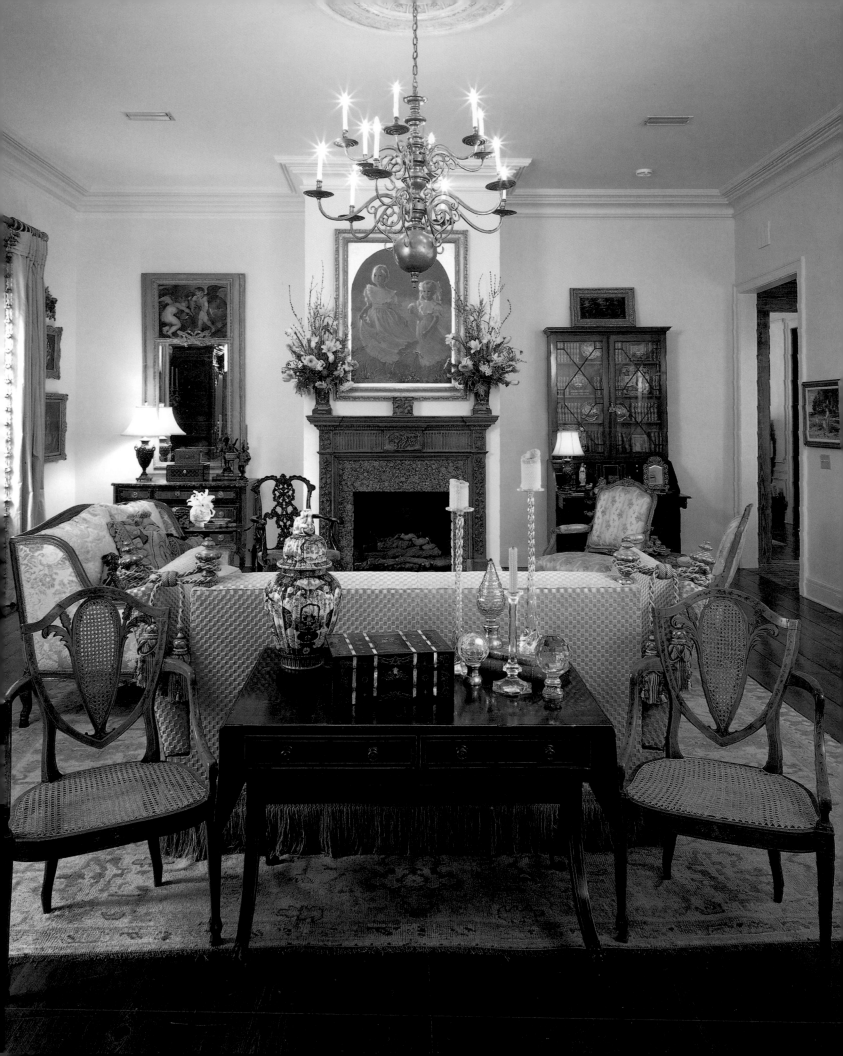

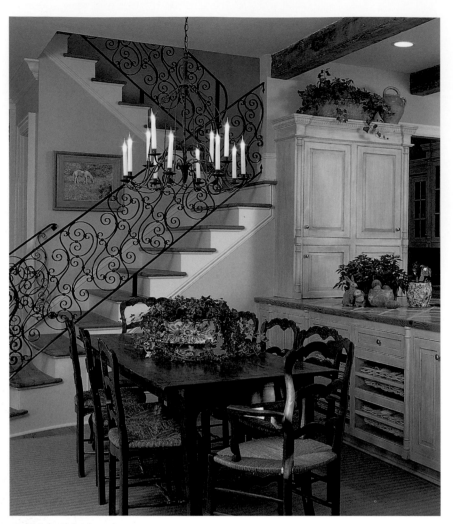

A subtle strié finish on the custom furniture-style cabinetry provides interest in this French country-style kitchen. The sinuous curves of the iron stair railing underscore the Gallic principle of beauty combined with utility.

Location: Ridgeland, Mississippi

[right] *Elegance and comfort dwell harmoniously in this formal sitting room. French and English antiques, contemporary artwork, and rich fabrics in mellow tints provide a quiet backdrop for the owner's collection of beautiful accessories.*

Location: Ridgeland, Mississippi

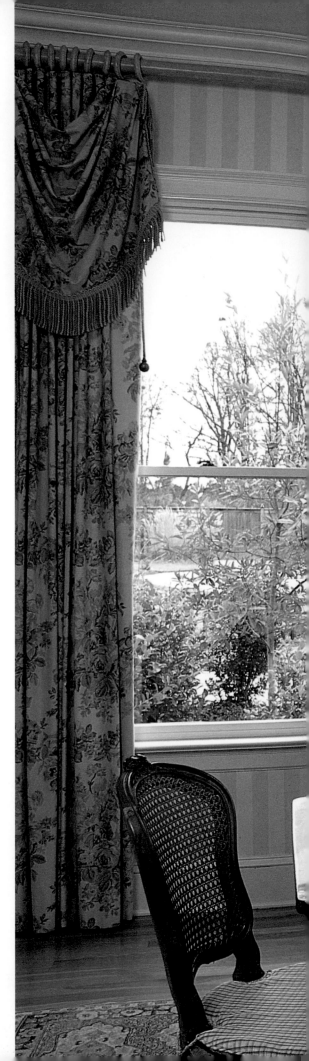

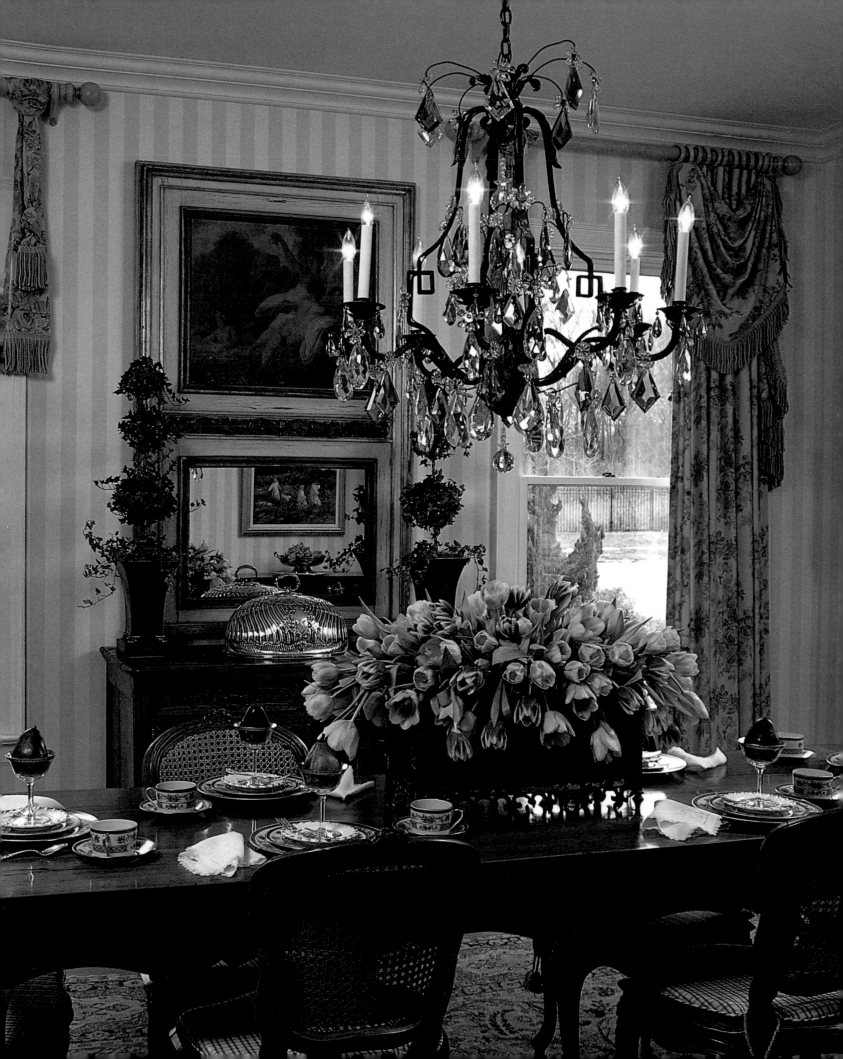

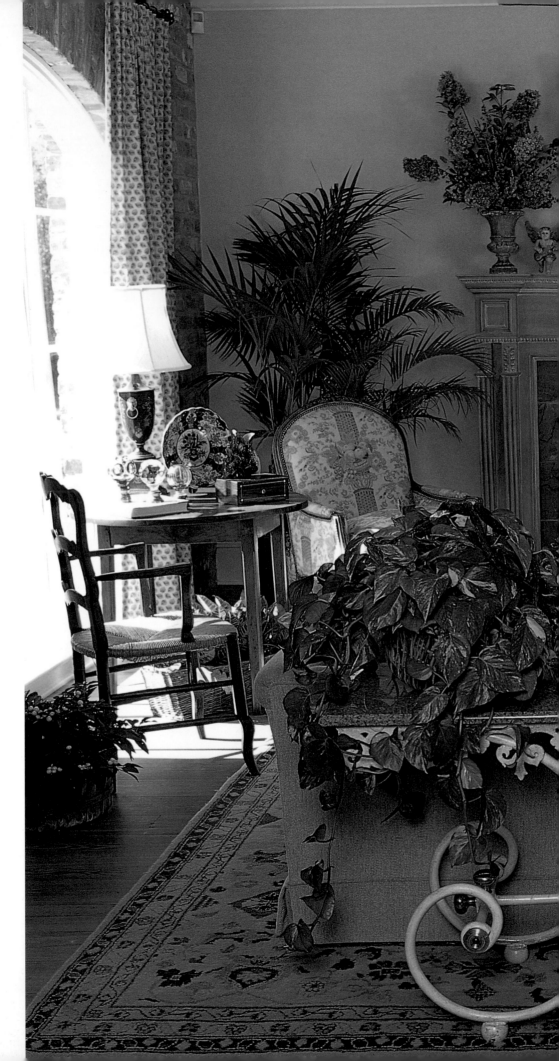

[right] *A patisserie table from Rouen, topped with a lamp fashioned from a Provincial pate crock, gives a bistro flavor to the space dividing family room from kitchen. An old brick wall adds rustic charm to this light-filled room.*

Location: Ridgeland, Mississippi

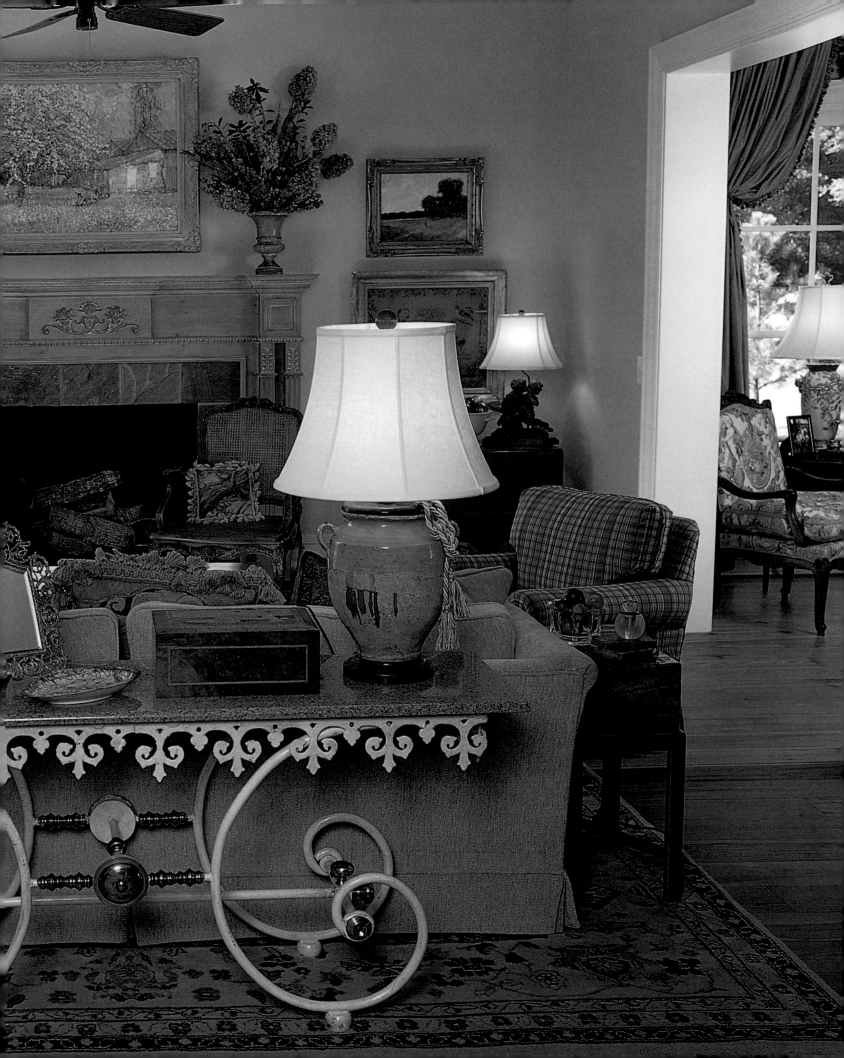

ANNELLE PRIMOS & ASSOCIATES

A designer's job is to interpret a client's ideas and needs and then create timeless and enduring interiors. Rooms should respect time-honored traditions and reflect the homeowner's personality and lifestyle.

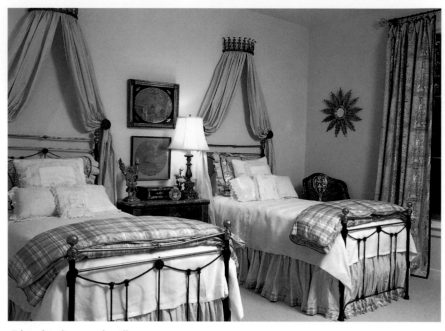

Edwardian linens and a silk bed-hanging soften these pair of antique black-iron beds to create the feel of a luxurious and peaceful guest retreat.

Location: Jackson, Mississippi

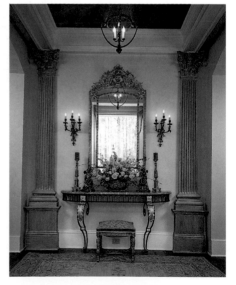

Antique carved-wood pilasters and a painted, domed ceiling framing this French iron console instill a sense of grandeur in this foyer.

Location: Jackson, Mississippi

[right] *Warm background colors and handsome French and English antiques create a refined and comfortable living room. Exposed beams and an elegant mantel layer the room with character.*

Location: Jackson, Mississippi

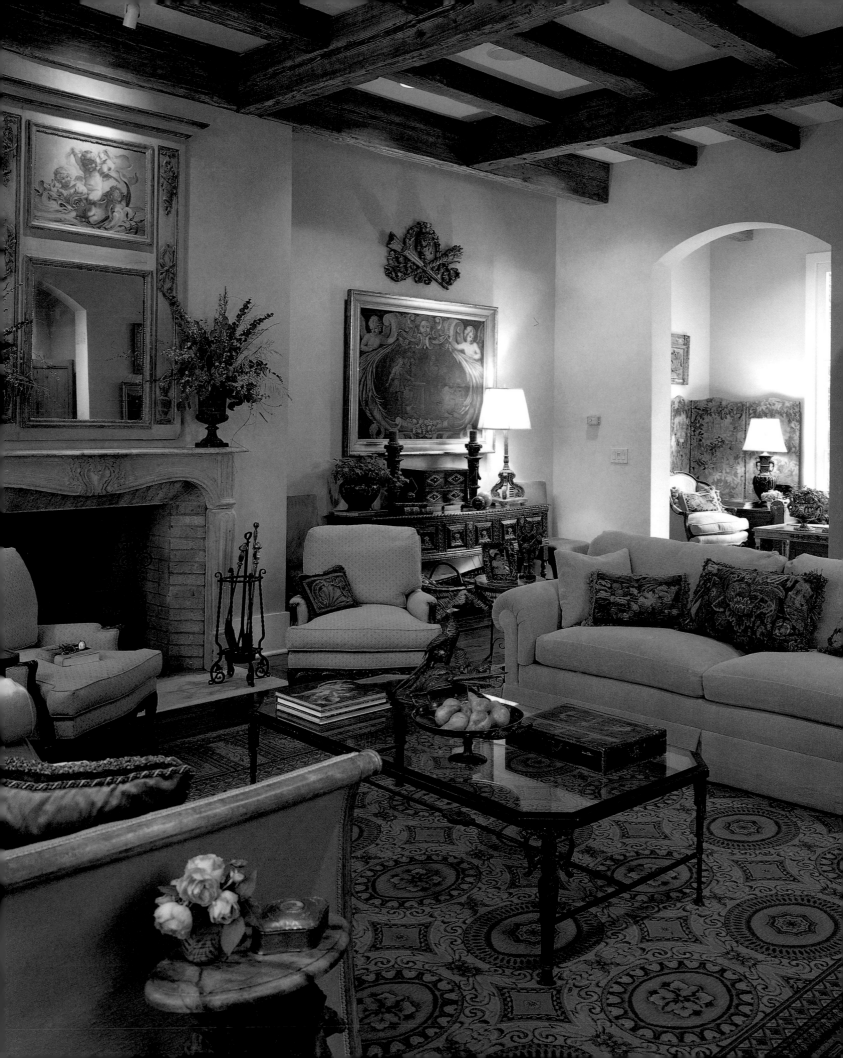

C. WEAKS INTERIORS

Rather than rely on a trademark look, C. Weaks Interiors endows each project with individuality based on the client's preferences, lifestyles, and requirements. The philosophy of the firm is based honest and ongoing communication between designer and client—a positive relationship that will result in a successful project. Despite the scope of the project or the size of the budget, quality, and distinction are always appropriate.

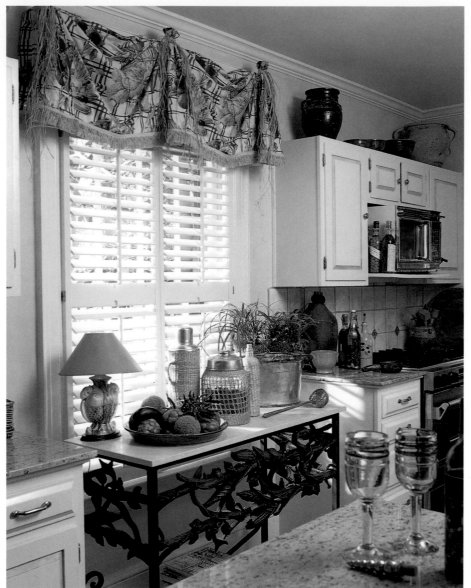

This older kitchen shows the benefits of a face-lift. While still smaller by today's standards, the efficient use of space and creative decorative elements combine to make an area that is enjoyable for both cooking and conversation. A unique iron console made from a gate of corn stalks serves as a decorative focal point and a practical spot for kitchen storage.

Location: Atlanta, Georgia

[right] *Contemporary art offers an interesting juxtaposition with antique accessories and European furnishings. A skirted table anchors the seating arrangement.*

Location: Atlanta, Georgia

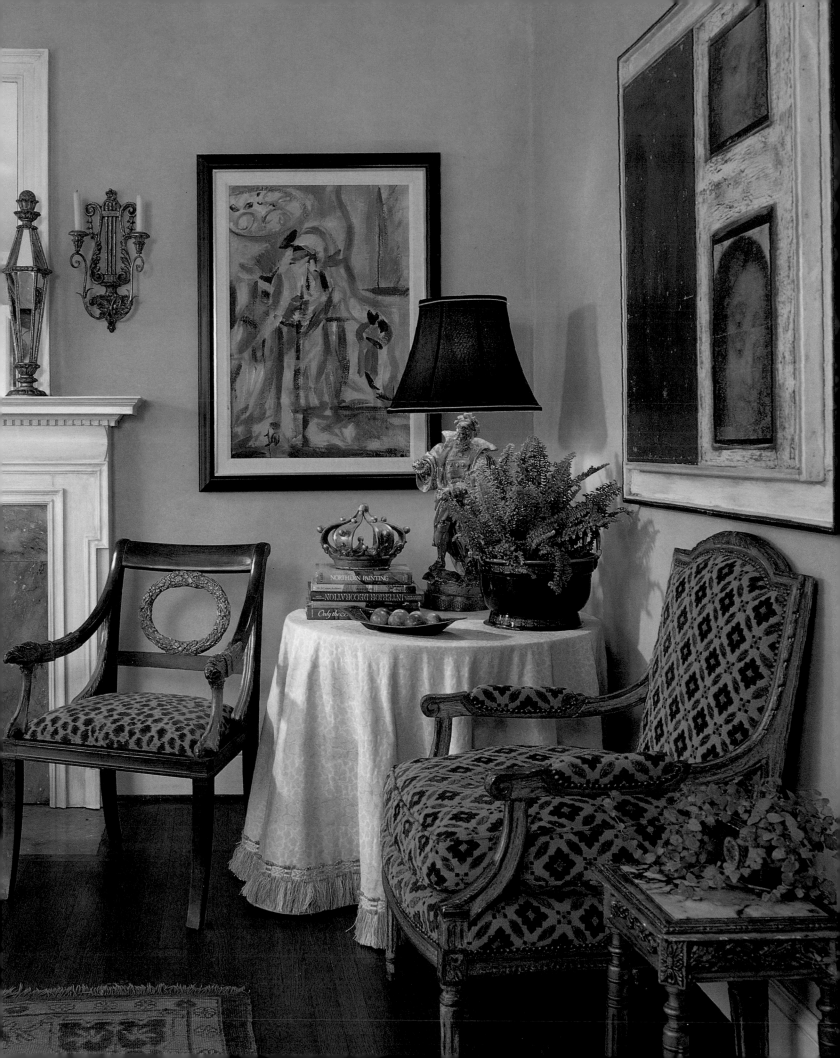

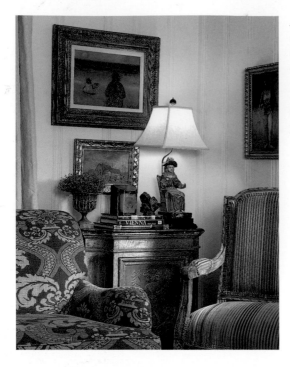

An interesting mix of art and accessories enlivens a corner of this library. Although much of the space is traditional with antiques and architectural objects, a work of contemporary abstract art adds color and vitality.

Location: Atlanta, Georgia

A sun-filled space links this family room to the outdoors. A woven sea-grass floor covering is practical and attractive for a high-traffic area. An unusual toile fabric with a pattern based on Christopher Columbus' arrival to America animates a set of chairs.

Location: Atlanta, Georgia

[right] The custom mantel enlivens this paneled library. An antique lion's face with the owner's initials provides a dramatic point over the fireplace in this intimate library.

Location: Atlanta, Georgia

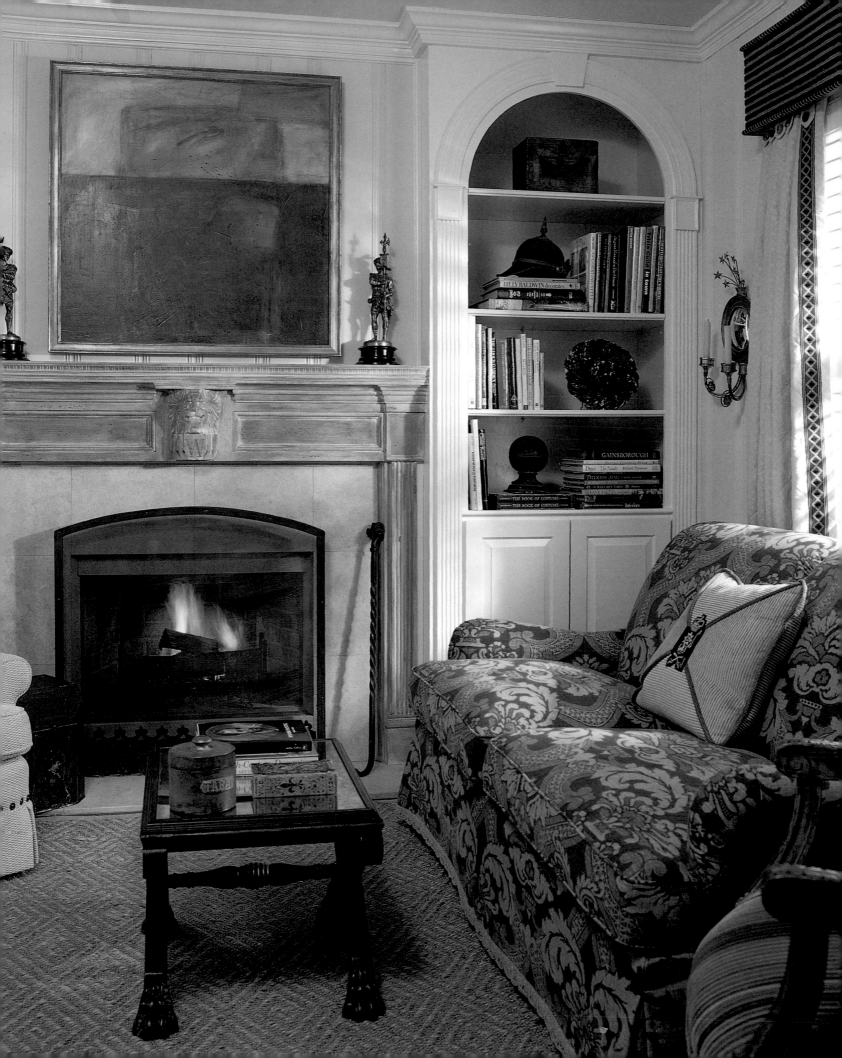

CHARME TATE INTERIORS

While this designer has clients of her own, in each of the projects shown here, her husband Ken Tate was the architect. Joining forces has been a positive influence on the designer. Each of these projects was designed from the ground up with attention to detail and obvious collaboration. Devotion to classical principles with a focus on the clients' desires enables the designer to create beautiful rooms that reflect the personality of the owner, possess comfortable elements, and provide balance and scale. Most people have a clear vision about their personal spaces; the designer is a channel for bringing those aspects to life. The designer sees the personal environment as not only a haven and refuge, but also an inspiration.

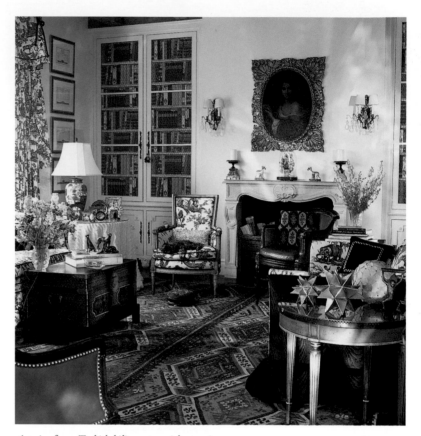

A pair of rare Turkish kilims sets a rich stage in this living room. A limestone mantle, black-and-white toile, a trompe-l'oeil library paper behind chicken wire, and an antique painting from Florence in a richly ornate frame all contribute to the room's eclectic mix.

Location: Madison, Mississippi

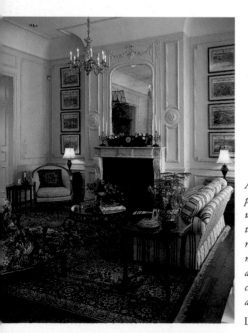

Antique, ivory-painted French paneling provides a subtle and elegant effect of unifying the many diverse elements in this living room. Stacking English aerial renderings by Kips, custom-designed metal coffee table by the decorator, an antique rug, a pair of commodes, and a custom-designed limestone mantel instill a distinctive look and feel in the space.

Location: Madison, Mississippi

[right] An heirloom dining table inspired the design of the elegant dining room. Cut velvet chair seats in a square design remain formal yet introduce a fresh note to the other more traditional furnishings in the room.

Location: Madison, Mississippi

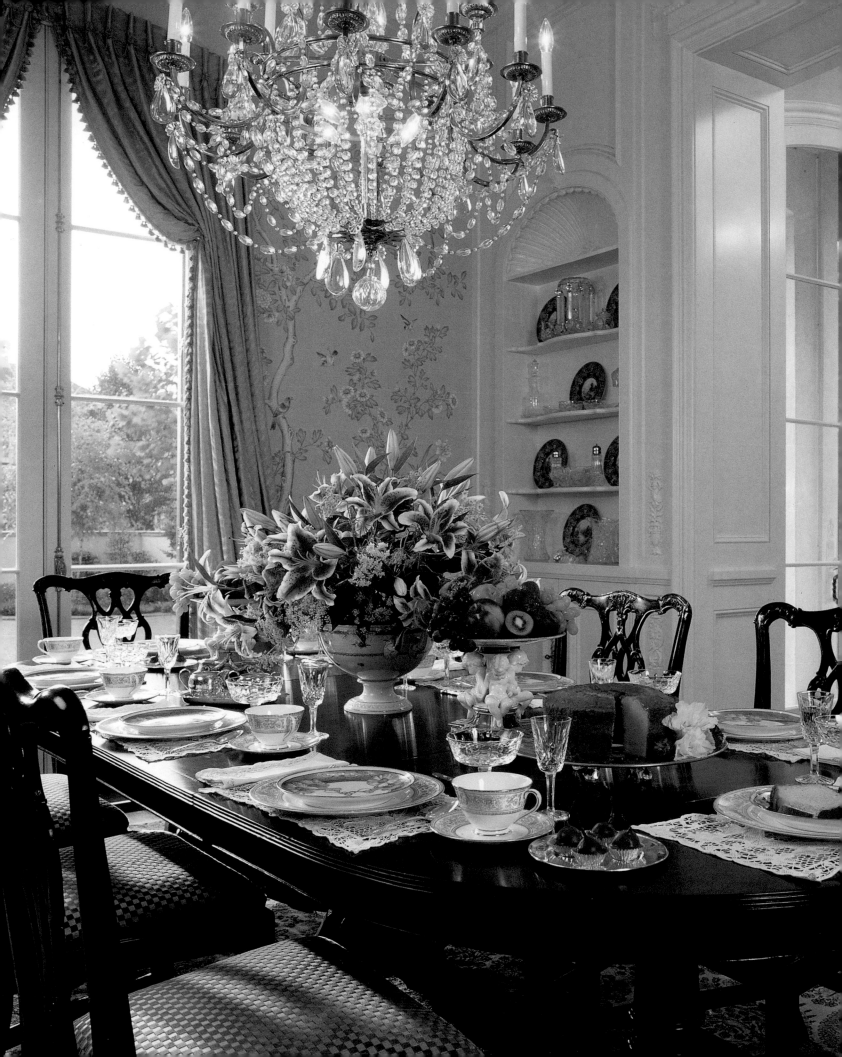

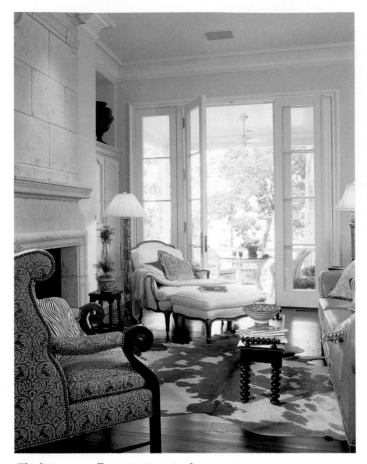

This living room offers an inviting mix of openness and classic proportions. A pair of sofas creates two intimate seating arrangements, while large, framed doorways provide a wonderful flow between rooms.

Location: Madison, Mississippi

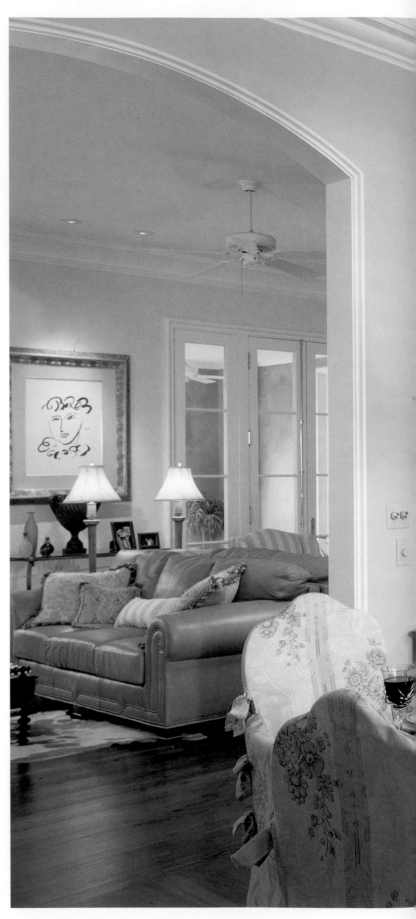

Timeless and sophisticated, this dining room is an engaging blend of classical details and pleasing proportion. A symmetrical arrangement of furniture, accessories centered on the sideboard, and an antique mirror reinforces the formality of the architecture.

Location: Madison, Mississippi

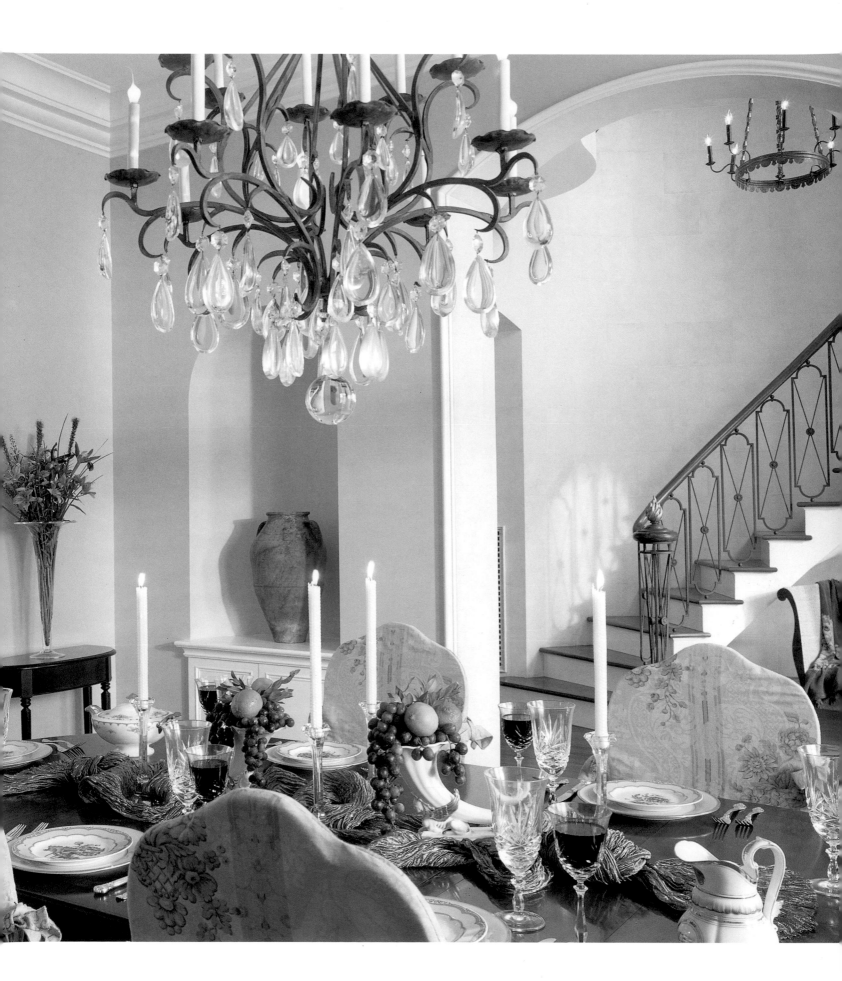

Checkerboard floor and green walls enliven this kitchen and adjacent breakfast room. Exposed beams and woven leather barstools counterpoint the neoclassical cabinets. Custom hand-painted tiles with a fruit motif and rustic pineapple sconces send a message of hospitality and welcome.

Location: Madison, Mississippi

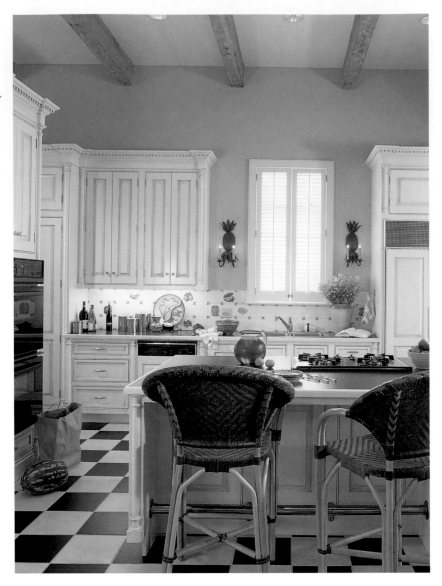

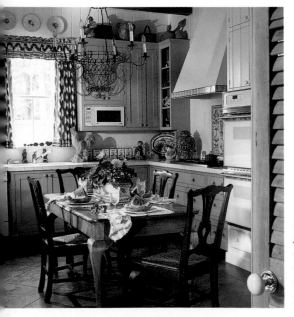

The primitive farmhouse kitchen contrasts to the more decorative living room. White-painted wooden walls and white tile offer a nice counterpoint to the Bermuda green cabinets. Blue and white fabric tiles and china add a decorative element.

Location: Madison, Mississippi

[right] *Fourteen-foot-tall ceilings with rough-hewn beams and a willow chandelier enliven the breakfast and sitting area. A large, arched opening with French doors and wide sidelights takes advantage of views to the lake.*

Location: Madison, Mississippi

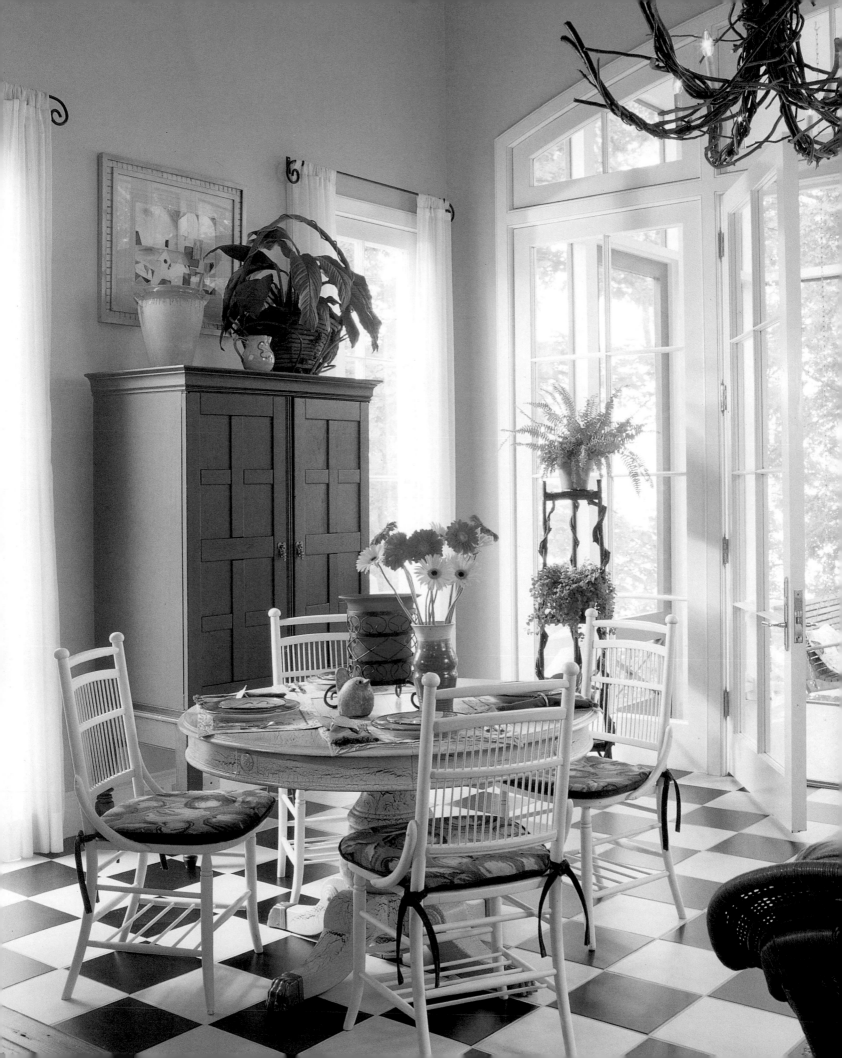

DANNY HARTLEY INTERIORS, INC.

Danny Hartley Interiors strives to give an aged presence to new surroundings by carefully integrating beloved possessions with new furnishings and accessories. Using impeccable choices in color and texture makes all of these details work together to present a complete and totally distinctive look; a look that is fascinating and alluring as well as comfortable and functional. This firm has been featured in several design publications, including *Southern Living* and *Veranda* magazine.

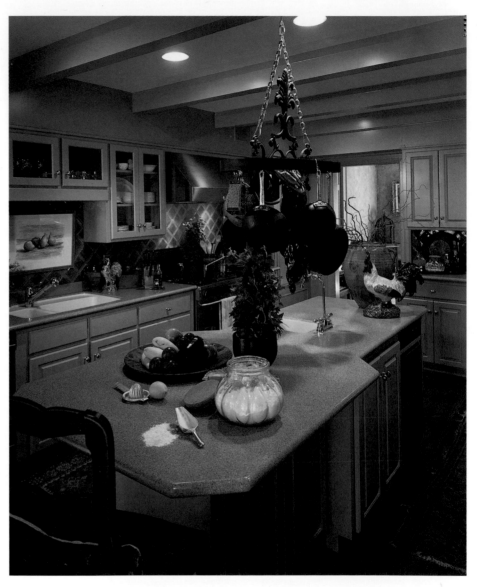

French country is the atmosphere; classic living is the order of the day in this newly renovated kitchen. Ceiling beams, traditional cabinetry in cream, and granite-like solid-surface countertops in almond are set apart by the dark sage walls, stainless-steel accessories, and a backsplash of diagonally set Italian tiles. Roosters and an iron pot rack add to the French-country flavor.

Location: Tuscaloosa, Alabama

[right] *The 18-foot fireplace wall stuccoed in monochromatic shades of olive serve as the perfect backdrop for the old Italian wrought-iron lighting fixtures and the oversized olive urns. The sofa, upholstered in a brilliant Scalamandre chenille, and the Tibet rug introduces color to the Mediterranean charm of this lovely room.*

Location: Tuscaloosa, Alabama

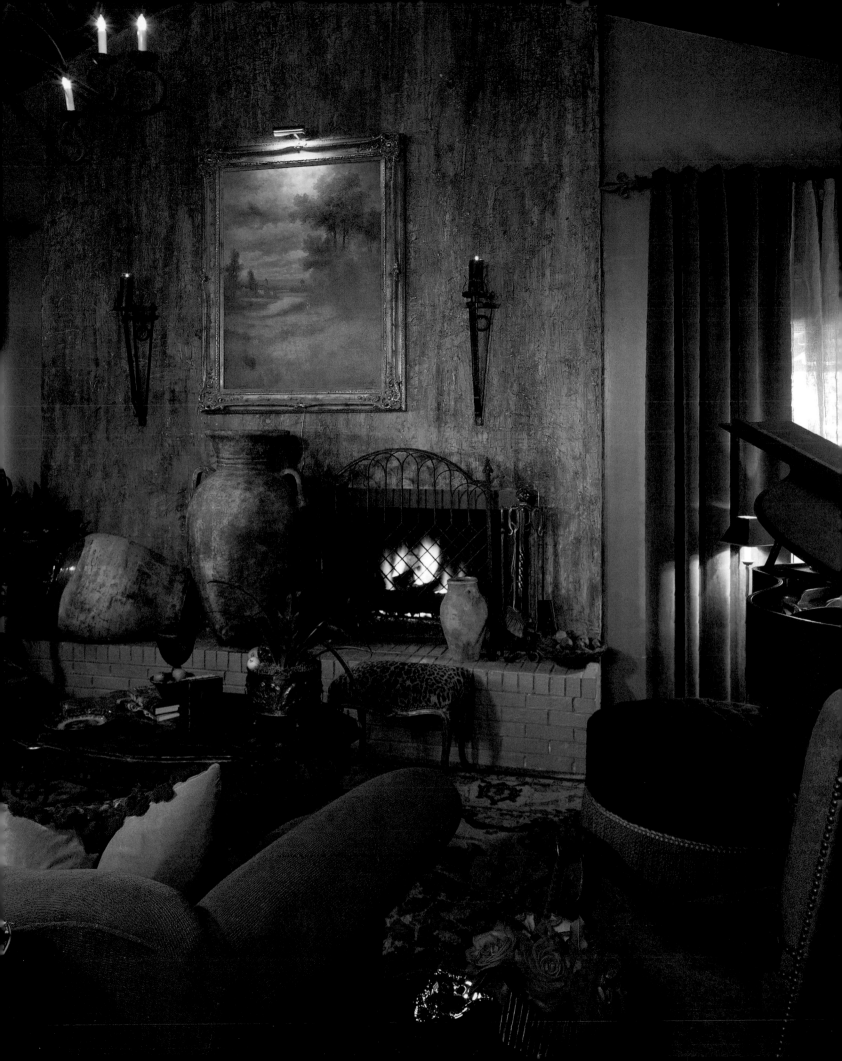

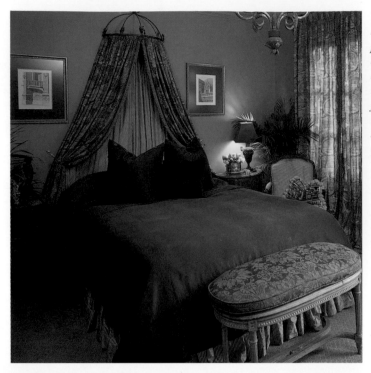

Taragon-colored walls and trellis-weave carpet help to create a soft, relaxed atmosphere in this inviting guest room. The chocolate silk duvet and parchment-and-chocolate bed hangings and window treatments lend themselves easily to this room filled with comfort. The eighteenth-century burled-wood commodes and antique lamps add to this room's beauty and charm.

Location: Tuscaloosa, Alabama

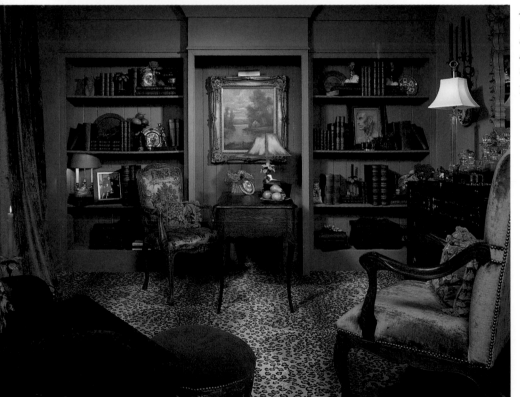

Antique furnishings and accessories combined with leopard-print carpet and custom-designed bookcases serve to create an avant-garde approach to design in this intimate study.

Location: Tuscaloosa, Alabama

[right] *The cognac glazed-stucco walls and fireplace serve as a richly appointed backdrop, transforming the east end of this elongated room into a cozy conversation area. Brightly colored pillows and kilim upholstered armchairs introduce color, while the iron-gate coffee table and antique shutters reflect the Mediterranean influence. Not seen are a billiard table and entertainment center at the west end that contribute to the easy, relaxed atmosphere of this downstairs recreation room.*

Location: Tuscaloosa, Alabama

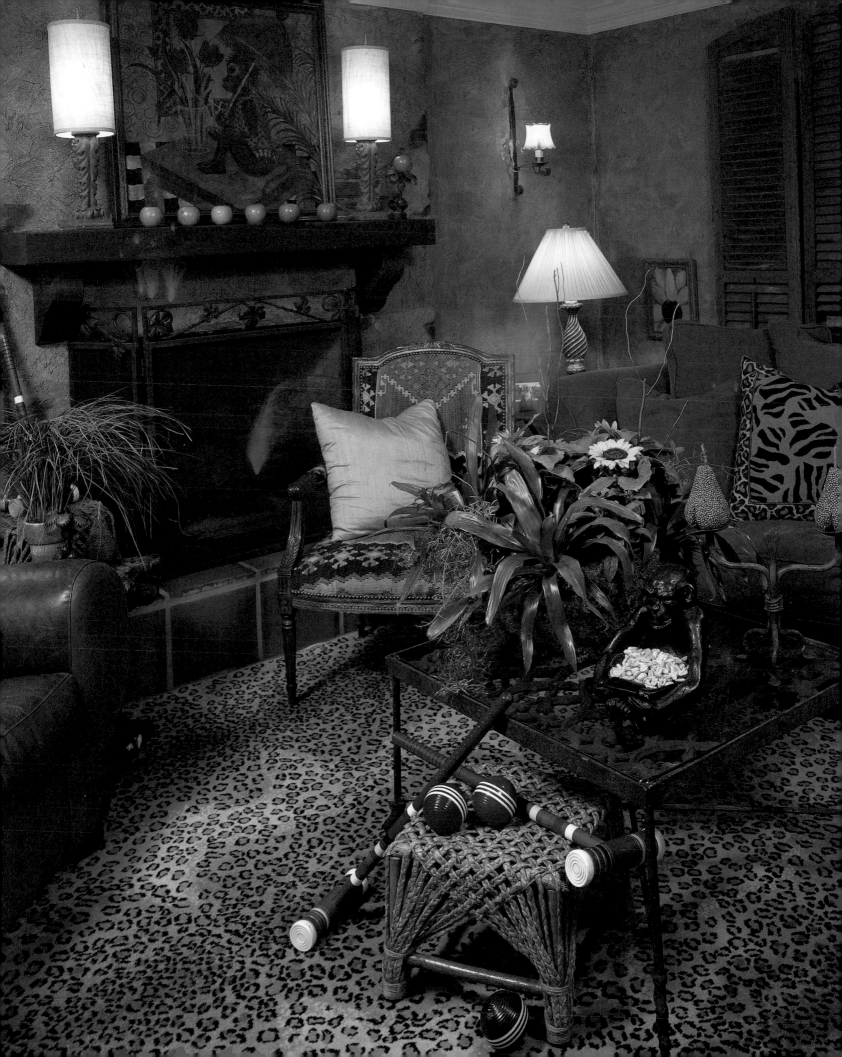

DAVID HOLCOMB INTERIORS

Always striving to achieve approachable, livable interiors, David Holcomb embraces the taste and requirements of his clients. Listening to a client's requirements is most important. The firm's ultimate goal is to individualize each project by interpreting the client's vision, tastes, and lifestyle into a beautiful and comfortable reality.

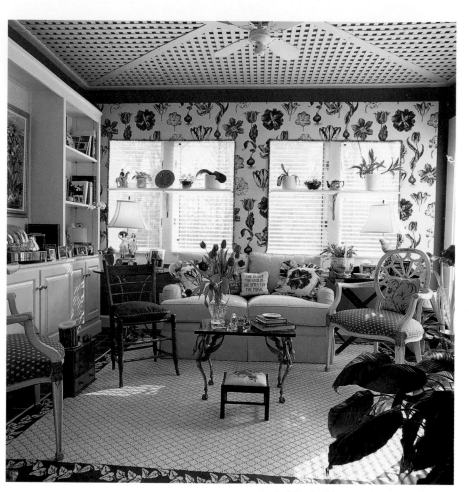

A colorful tulip fabric sets the tone for this light and airy garden room. A built-in cabinet offers practical storage and display to ensure the room will be a popular gathering spot.

Location: Atlanta, Georgia

A custom-made headboard with a Chippendale design instills a masculine feel for this master bedroom. English antiques and comfortable-upholstered pieces enhance the room's tranquil sense of enclosure.

Location: Atlanta, Georgia

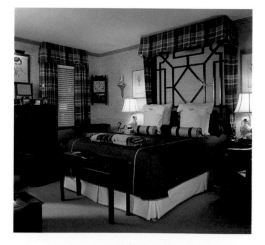

This elegant dining room radiates from the hand-painted wall-covering to a custom-made rug. Lacquered Queen Anne chairs are accented with gold leaf. A collection of eighteenth-century teapots enlivens a mirrored wall.

Location: Atlanta, Georgia

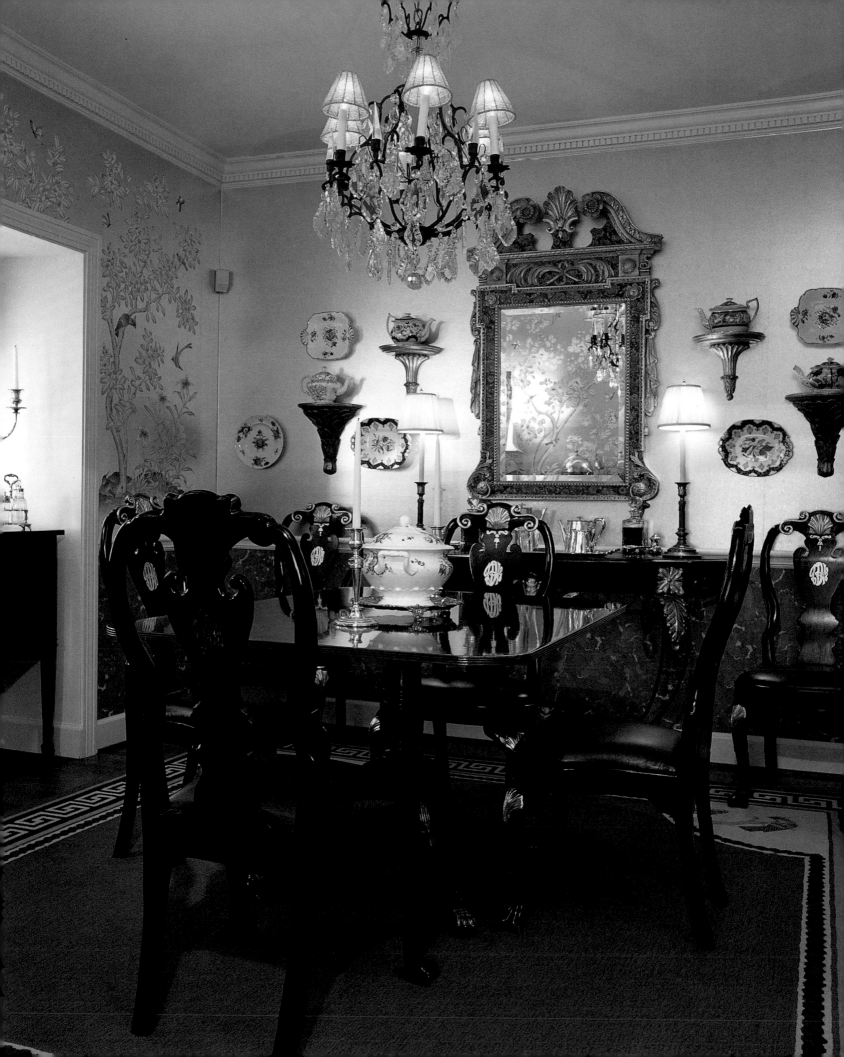

G. S. HINSEN COMPANY

Established ten years ago, G. S. Hinsen Company earned the reputation as a local source for fine European antiques, quality reproductions, and unusual accessories. The firm specializes in residential and commercial design, drawing inspiration from Continental influences. Each individual client's lifestyle and interests are reflected in the firm's approach to creating a design concept. G. S. Hinsen strives for classic, timeless interior design with an emphasis on quality and attention to detail.

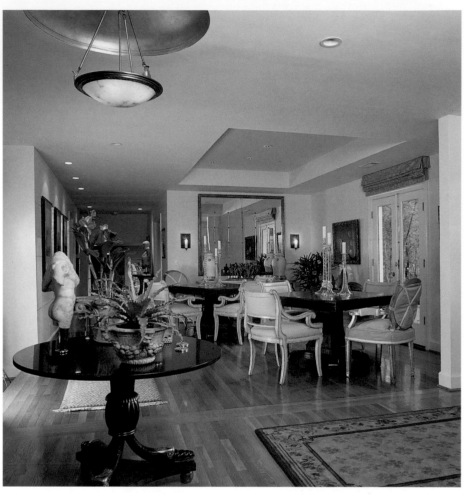

This thoughtfully proportioned space serves as a foyer, gallery, and dining area. The furniture is arranged to enhance the architectural details.

Location: Nashville, Tennessee

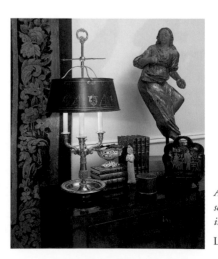

A Biedermeier chest offers the perfect setting for a variety of accessories including a gilded Santos.

Location: Nashville, Tennessee

[right] A pastoral Flemish tapestry offers a dramatic backdrop for this exquisite seating area. An eclectic mix of furniture and accessories add another layer of sophistication to the room.

Location: Nashville, Tennessee

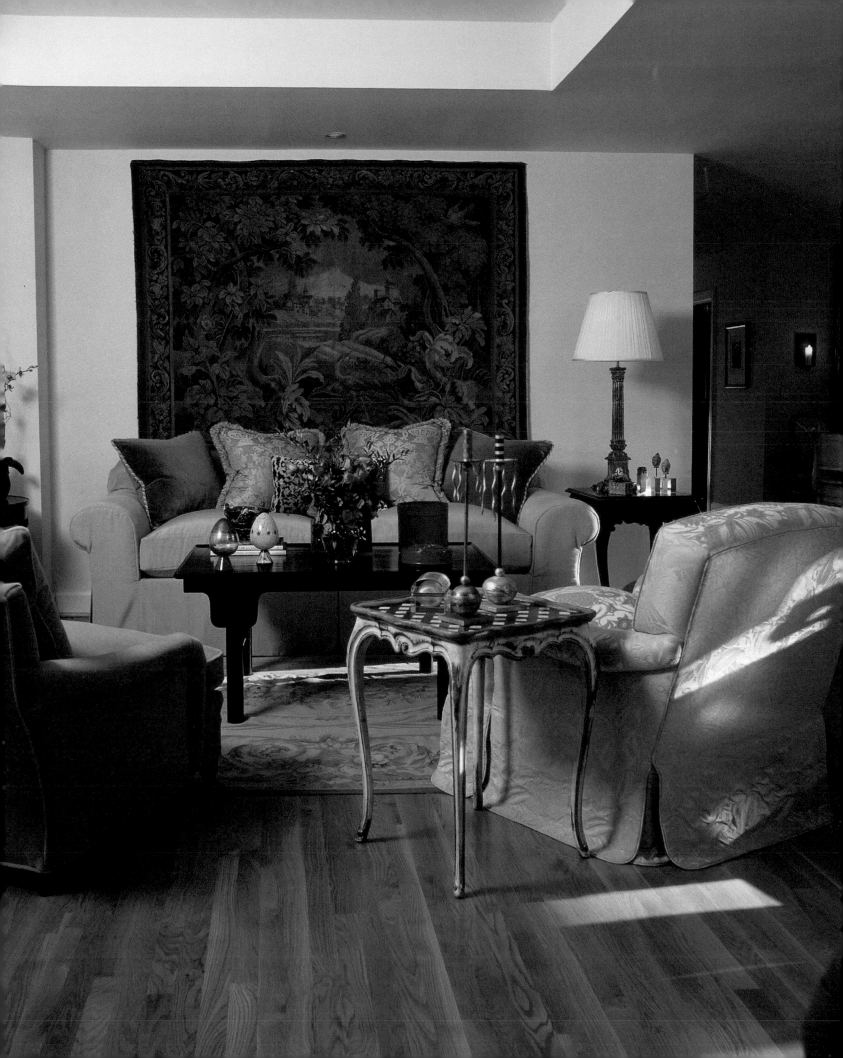

*Dramatic pyramidal cabinets and the inter-
play of sumptuous fabrics instill formality in
this lady's library. Floor-to-ceiling windows
flood the space with natural light.*

Location: Nashville, Tennessee

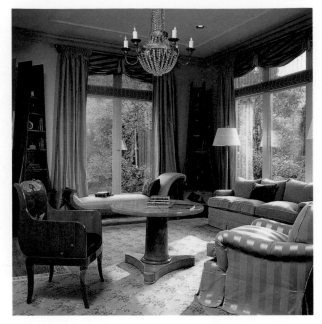

*A subtle, monochromatic color scheme establishes
a pleasing ambiance for period artwork.*

Location: Nashville, Tennessee

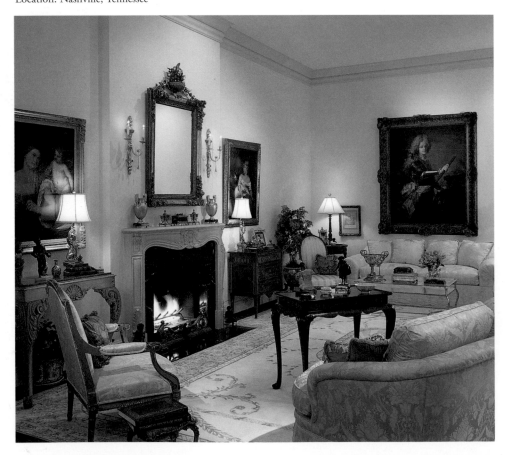

[right] *This ambitious and
utterly engaging breakfast
room is a reservoir of fine
European antiques.*

Location: Nashville,
Tennessee

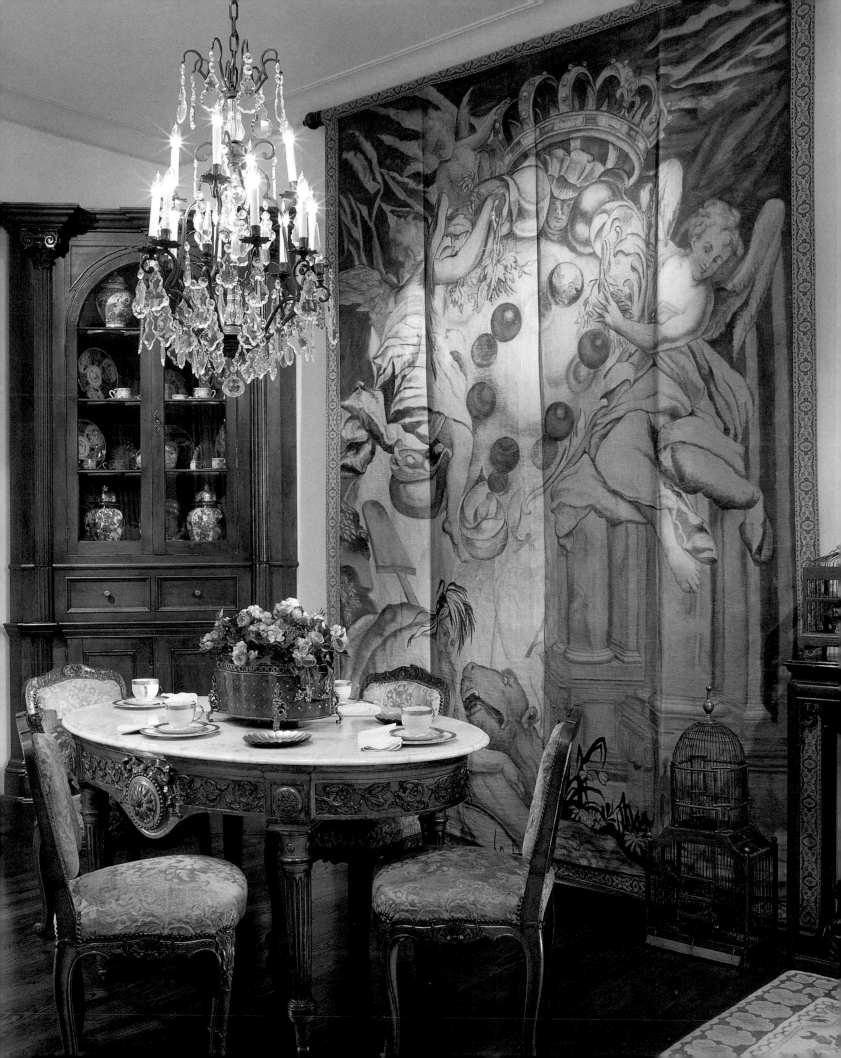

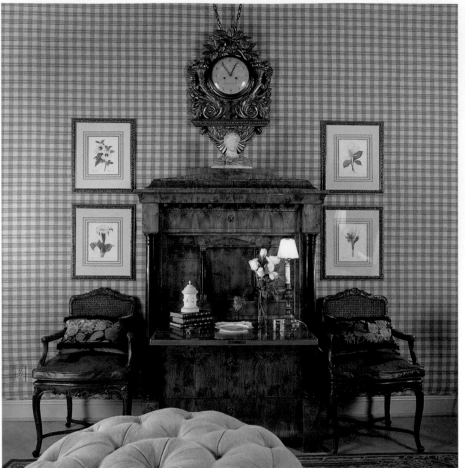

An upholstered wall provides an engaging backdrop for a Russian Biedermeier secretary and a nine-teenth-century Swedish wall clock.

Location: Nashville, Tennessee

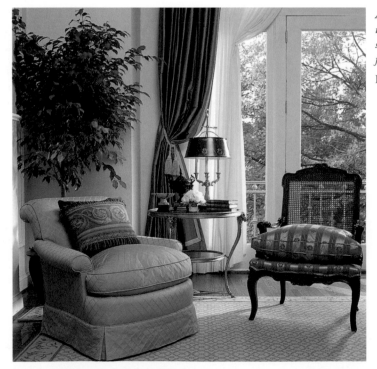

A period gueridon table anchors the corner of a tranquil conver-sation area. Elegant draperies frame a large expanse of glass.

Location: Nashville, Tennessee

The European ambiance of this intimate keeping room is heightened by the incorpora-tion of trompe-l'oeil to emphasize the distinctive architectural features.

Location: Nashville, Tennessee

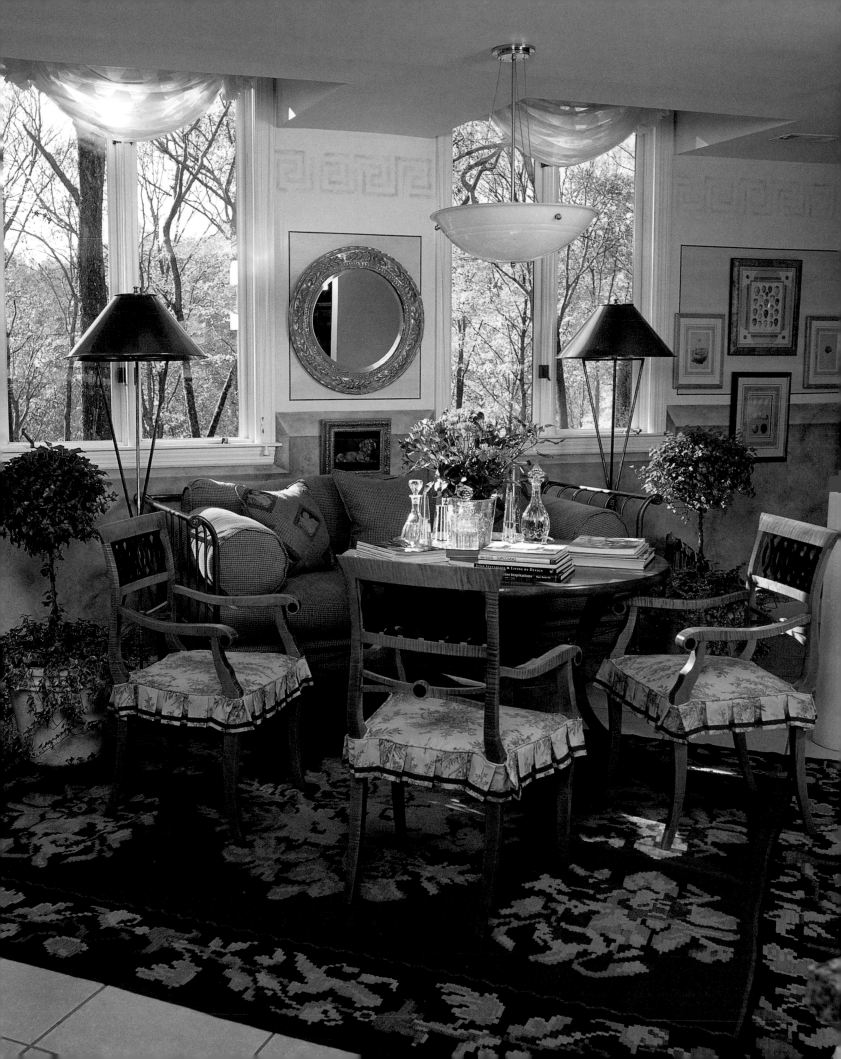

JO EMMERT INTERIOR DESIGN

Grounded in the traditional and decorative arts, Jo Emmert is known for redefining the classics. With an emphasis on architecture, color, and proportion, the firm's goal is to create a discriminating design that has a sense of permanence, comfort, and continuity. Understanding the functional needs, personal habits, and individual tastes of the clients is of the utmost importance. Working together, the designer helps clients achieve surroundings that make them feel good about their investment, make family and friends comfortable, and refresh the spirit as well.

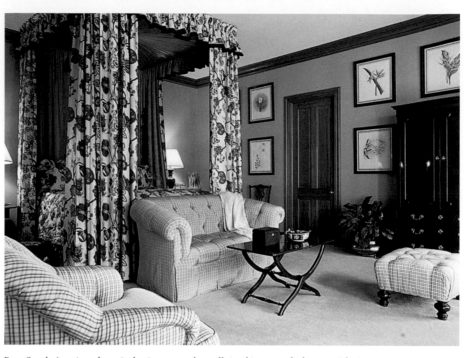

Rare South American botanical prints cover the walls in this master bedroom, with views to a courtyard garden. Bed hangings are from the ceiling with a traditional sunburst tester. A putty and vermilion-red, Jacobean chintz, accented with sage and black, complement a classic cotton taffeta plaid on upholstered furniture.

Location: Baton Rouge, Louisiana

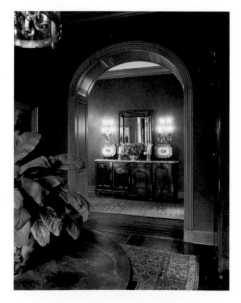

[right] *Terra-cotta–textured walls in this formal entrance lead the way to the vestibule by way of a paneled cypress arch. A marble-topped French buffet is overlooked by a spectacular antique English mirror. Crystal sconces are paired with English porcelain chargers on stands.*

Location: Baton Rouge, Louisiana

An inviting cypress architectural wall sets the tone for this engaging space, while the antique Serapis rug dictates the color scheme. Neutral silk damask draperies, French wing chairs, and fauteuils create a welcoming and comfortable salon.

Location: Baton Rouge, Louisiana

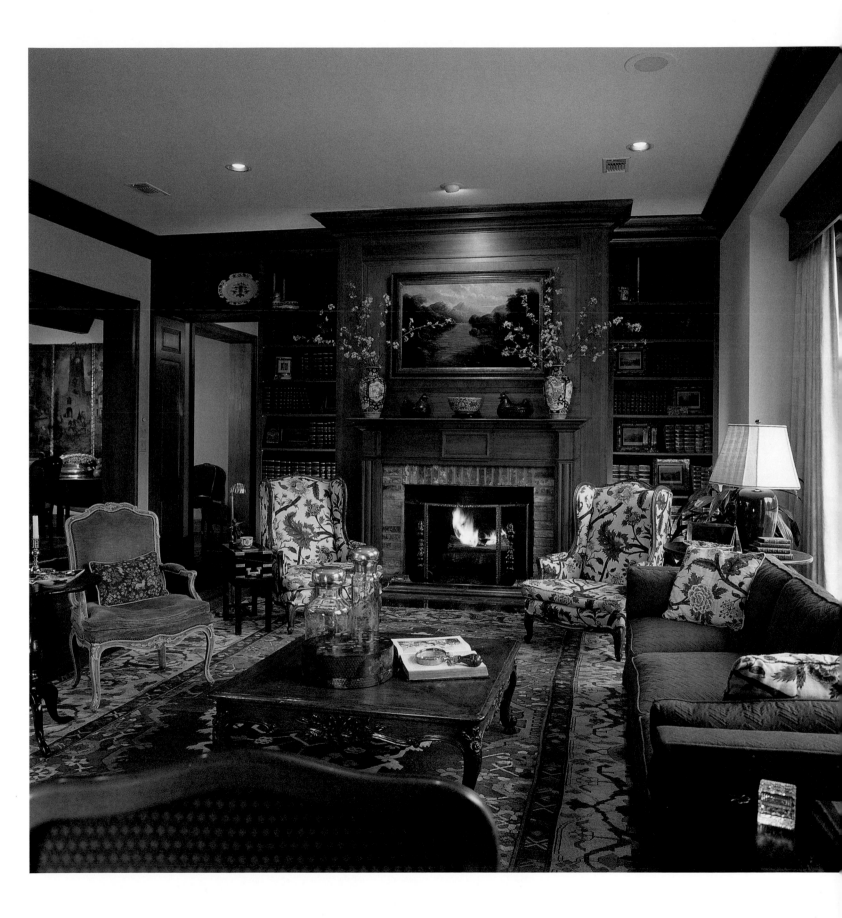

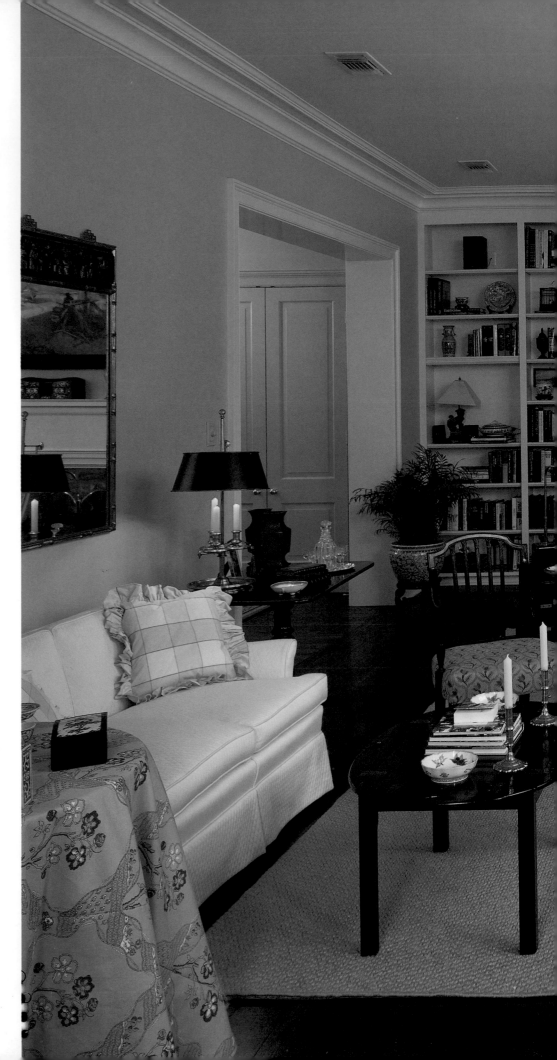

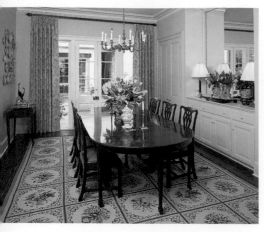

*With storage as a paramount concern
in this French townhouse, custom
built-ins accommodate dining-room
appointments. French doors with sidelights and custom-dyed French documentary linen draperies lead to a
courtyard. English antique dining
table and chairs and Oriental porcelain are relaxed with a Portuguese
needlepoint rug.*

Location: Baton Rouge, Louisiana

[right] *A French townhouse with sunny,
informal fabrics and sisal rug invites
one to be comfortable amid English
antiques and Oriental porcelain. White
quilted cotton covers the sofas and com-
pliments a yellow cotton taffeta plaid
used for chairs and pillows. The printed
French linen draperies were custom
dyed to match a documentary fabric.*

Location: Baton Rouge, Louisiana

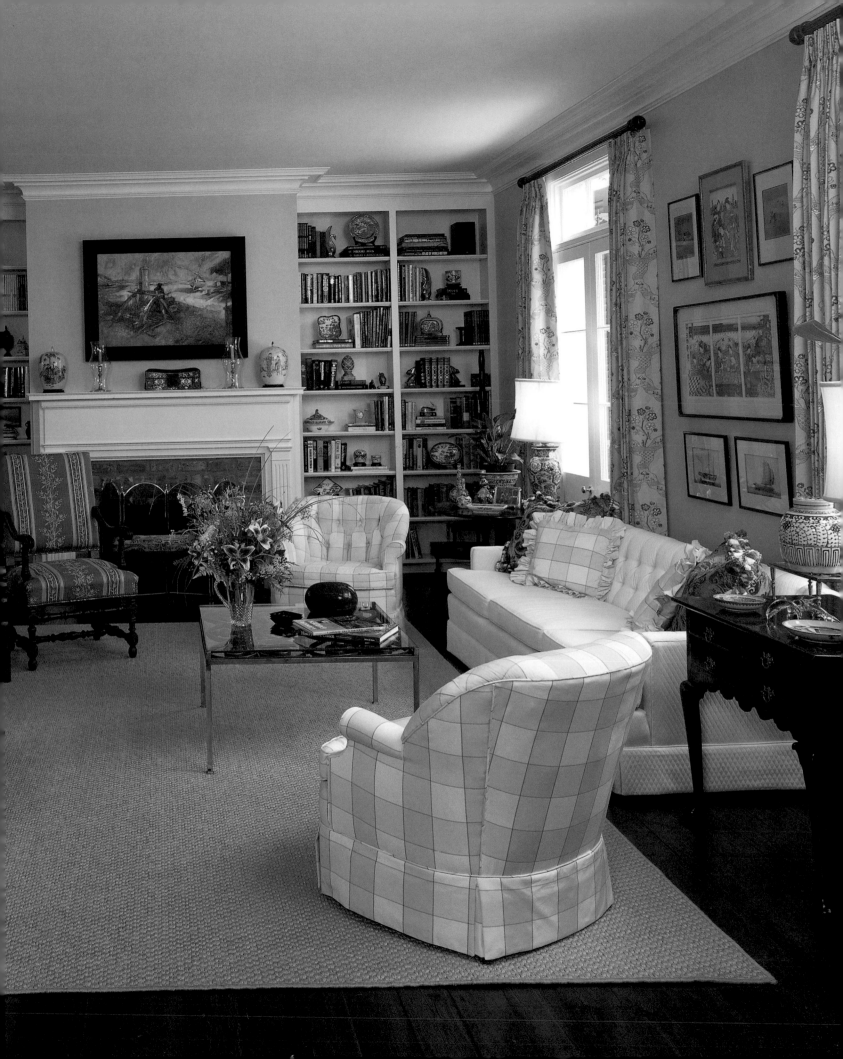

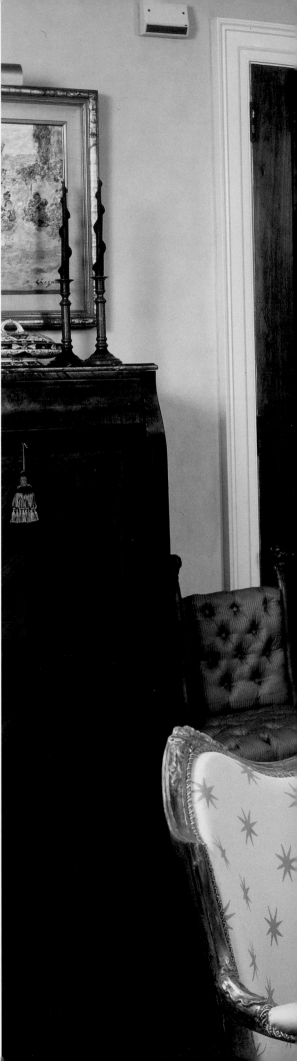

DISTILLING THE ESSENCE

LANDY GARDNER INTERIORS

Landy Gardner Interiors' diverse clientele requires a diverse approach to design. How a client works, plays, entertains, and relaxes all must be taken into account when designing and decorating interiors. Although an individual room is but a portion of the entire home, in the context of the whole, each room must possess its own unique, yet unifying, essence. Good design blends old and new, things familiar and things fresh, techniques proven and techniques untried.

[right] *A custom-built piano by Storrie and Clark for a riverboat captain anchors one corner of the room. Vermicelli Graufage fabric on the sofas was made in Italy.*

Location: Nashville, Tennessee

A sophisticated window seat anchors an inviting seating area in the bedroom.

Location: Nashville, Tennessee

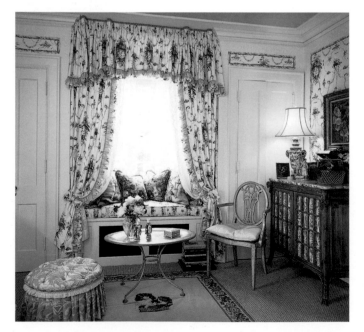

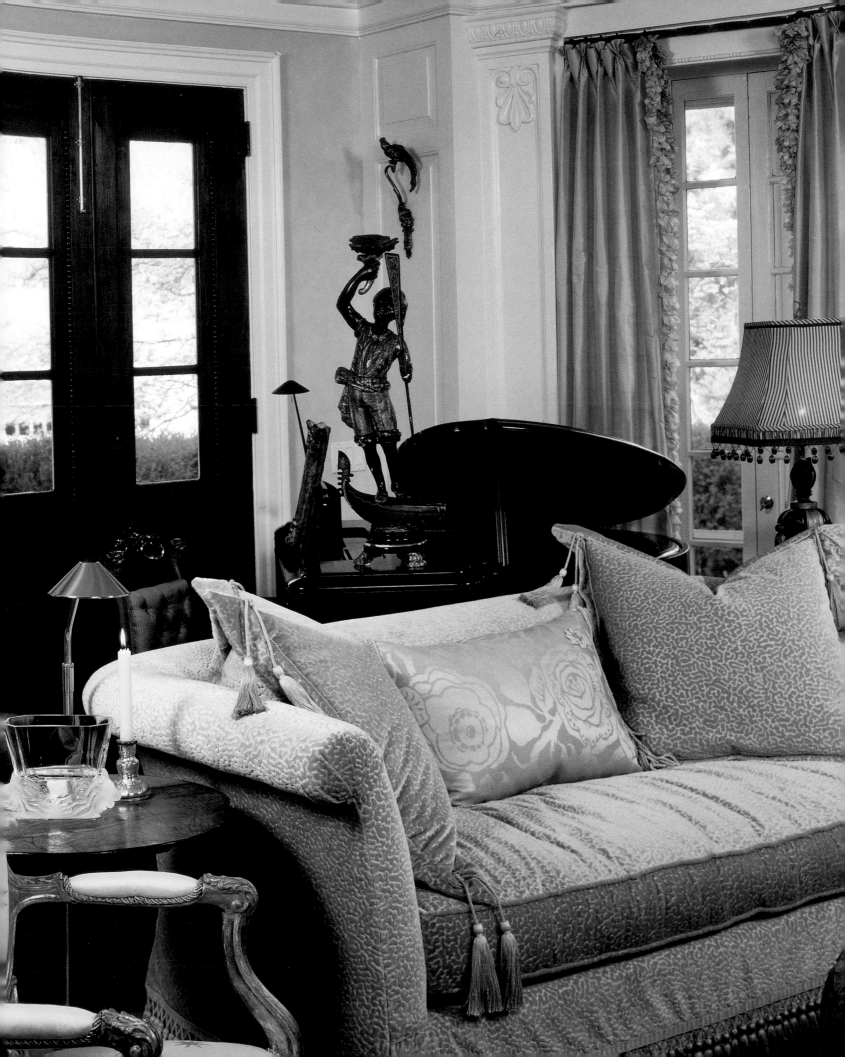

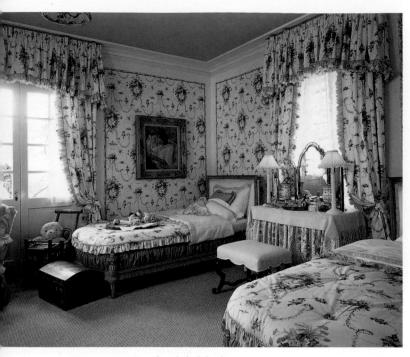

Vintage 1920s French-style beds lend scale and comfort in this romantic bed-room. For drama, the same pattern is repeated for window treatments, walls, and bedcoverings.

Location: Nashville, Tennessee

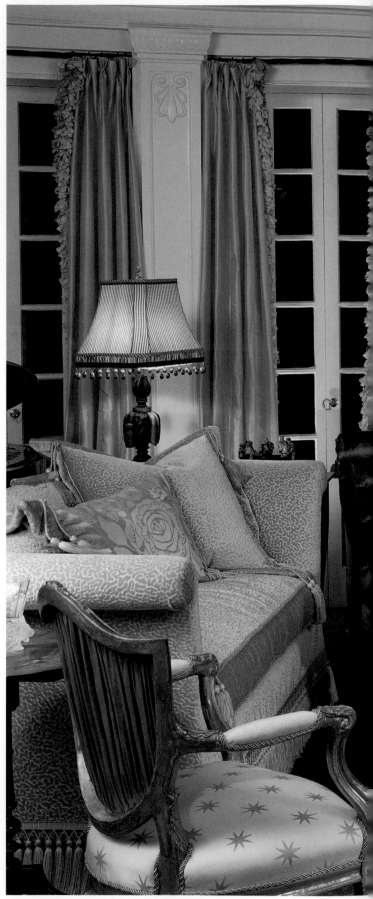

A curved wall of windows offers a striking background for this room. The furniture arrangement accentuates the sweeping geometry. A nineteenth-century tapestry covers a circular ottoman that fits together in four pieces.

Location: Nashville, Tennessee

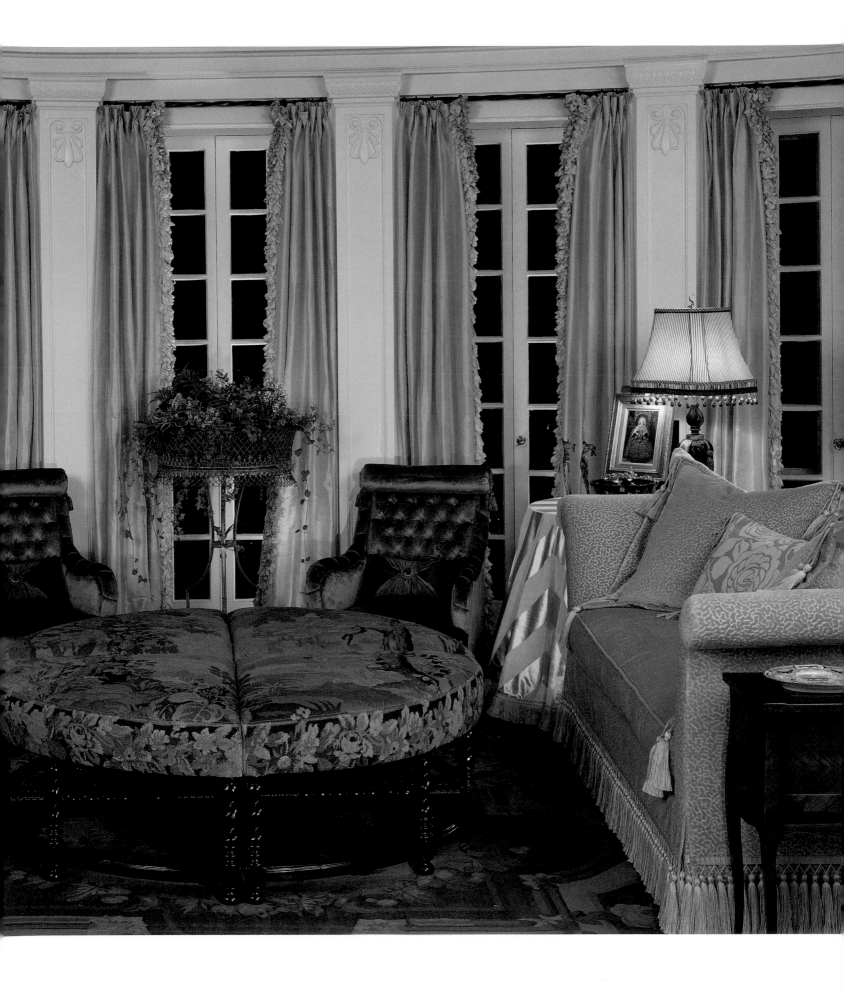

LEO DOWELL INTERIORS, INC.

Leo Dowell Interiors' design philosophy is simple—drama and sensuality. When he chooses an object, it is part of a symphony. Every note adds to the complete concert, yet each item on its own may be unexpected. The designer creates a dusting of the centuries by mixing natural stones, strong architectural accents, heavy textures, and classic European antiques. The firm takes inspiration from a variety of sources, from world travels as well as from the big screen.

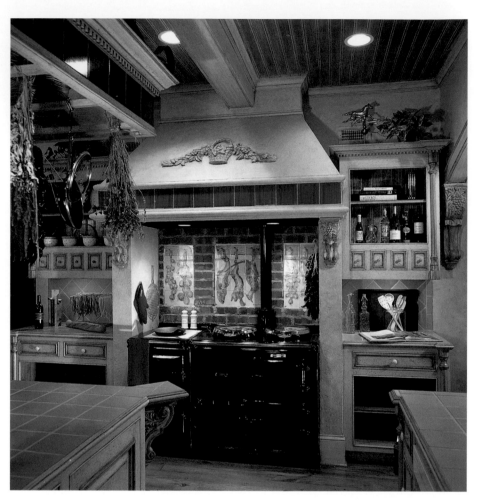

Hand-painted Portuguese tiles enliven an old brick wall above the stove to enhance this kitchen's old-world charm.

Location: Charlotte, North Carolina

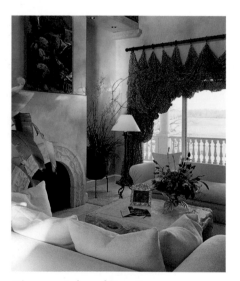

The unexpected use of Desert Storm camouflage (original tank covers) provides a striking window treatment in this living room designed for a young couple.

Location: Catawba, North Carolina

[right] *A wonderful mix of natural materials, handworn surfaces, rich textures, and worm-distressed finishes instills character in a Country French kitchen.*

Location: Charlotte, North Carolina

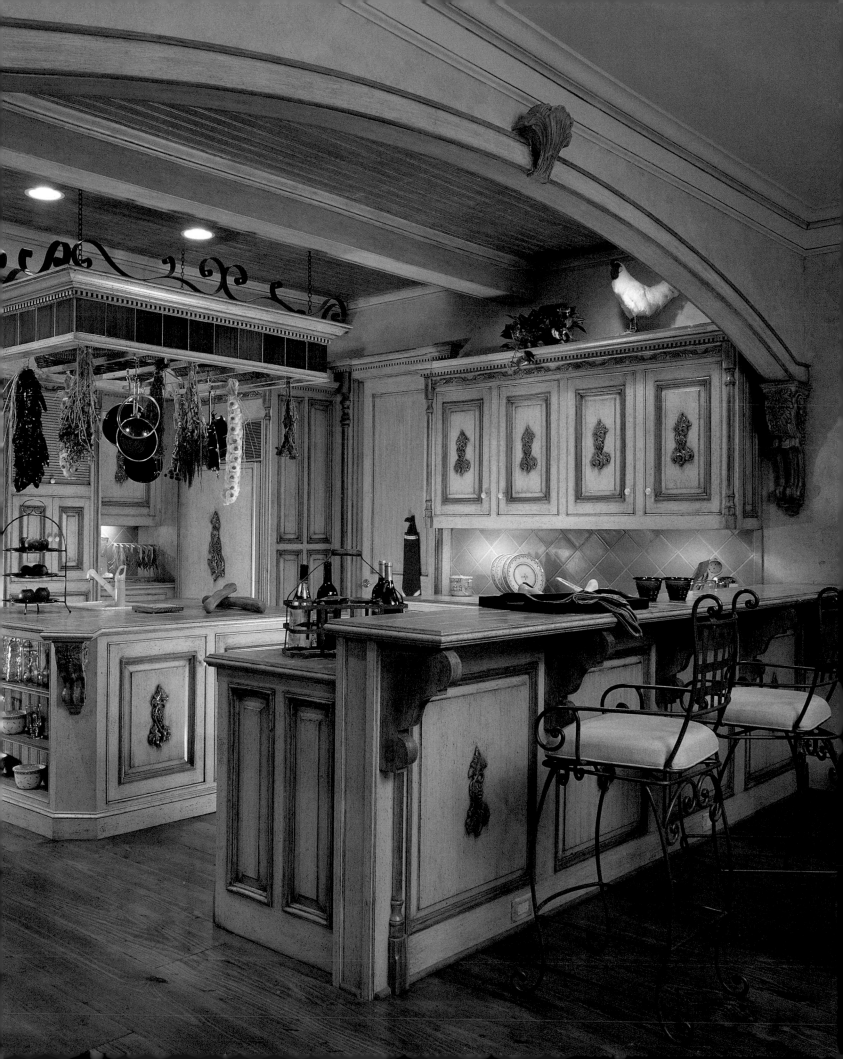

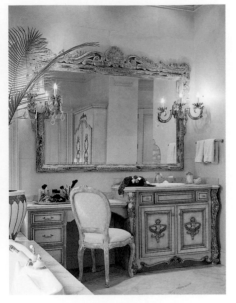

Custom cabinetry designed and manufactured by Leo Dowell adds elegance to this master bathroom. The large mirror and finely detailed woodwork appear to date from the seventeenth century.

Location: Hamptonville, North Carolina

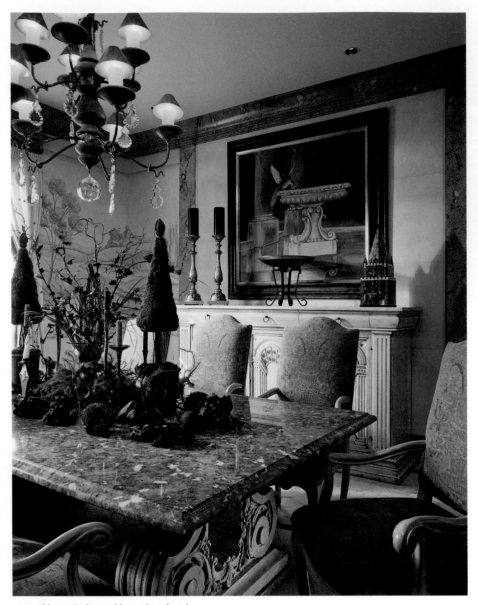

A marble-top Italian table combined with tapestry chairs and a hand-painted mural create a theatrical dining experience. Tall ceilings and ornate architectural detailing magnify the room's sense of drama.

Location: Hamptonville, North Carolina

[right] *The walls of a boy's bedroom appear to have been transplanted from an old monastery with a leaky roof. Fifteen yards of safari cloth envelope a French-style daybed to create an inviting and dramatic cocoon.*

Location: Charlotte, North Carolina

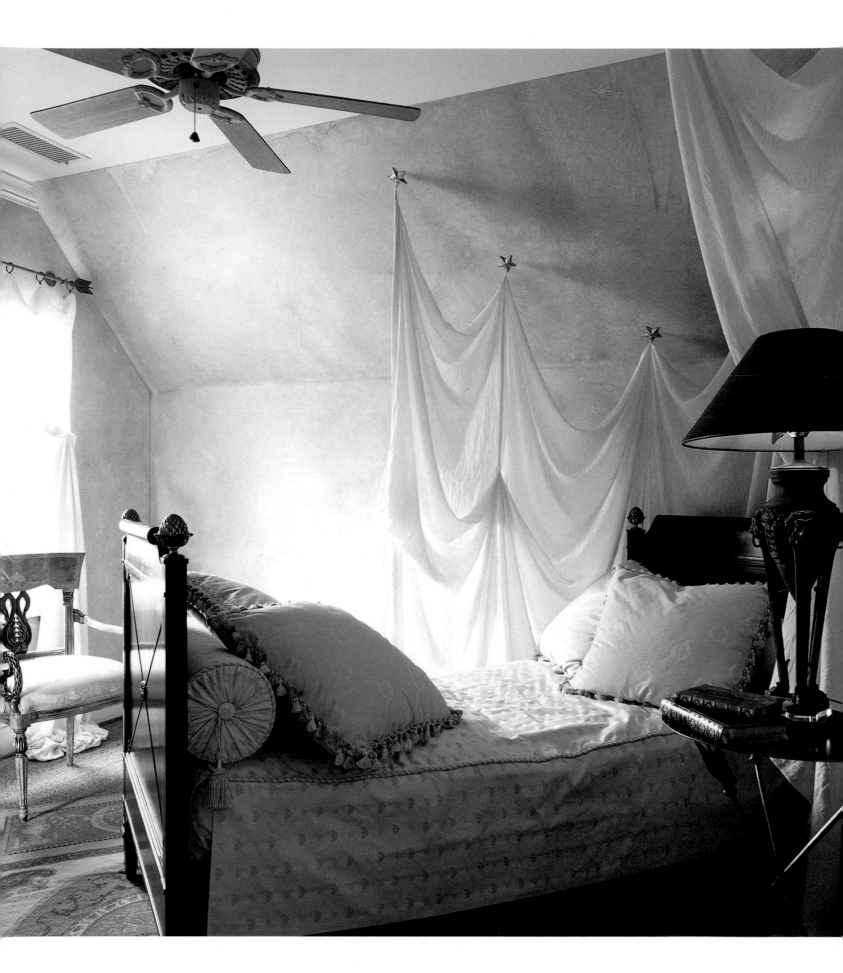

SANFORD R. THIGPEN, INTERIORS, INC.

A successful design project begins and ends with the client. The firm has years of experience helping clients make decisions and creating timeless environments. Each project is an ongoing discussion of ideas on the mood and essence of the room and the client's own lifestyle. Continual involvement along every step of the way results in a finished product as individual as the people involved.

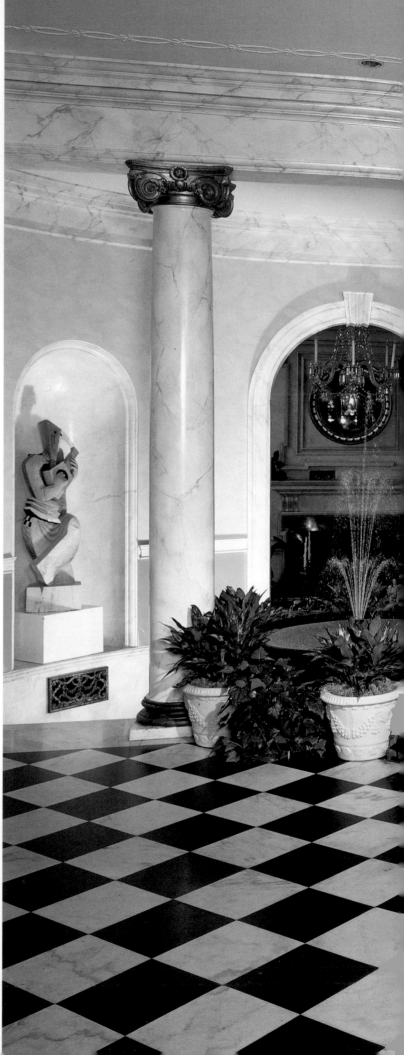

[right] *Elegance is the hallmark of this restored nineteenth-century home in Atlanta. A palette of soft blues and warm yellows and a new fountain imbues the foyer with sensation of a European garden room.*

Location: Atlanta, Georgia

Vanilla creme walls and serene salmon hues—tempered with coffee and Prussian-blue accents—create an elegant, yet comfortable living room. Tailored and meticulously upholstered furnishings express a sense of timeless refinement.

Location: Atlanta, Georgia

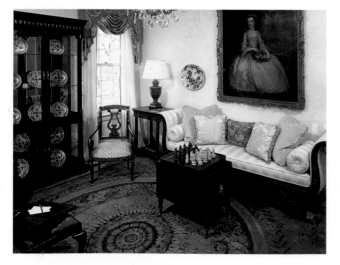

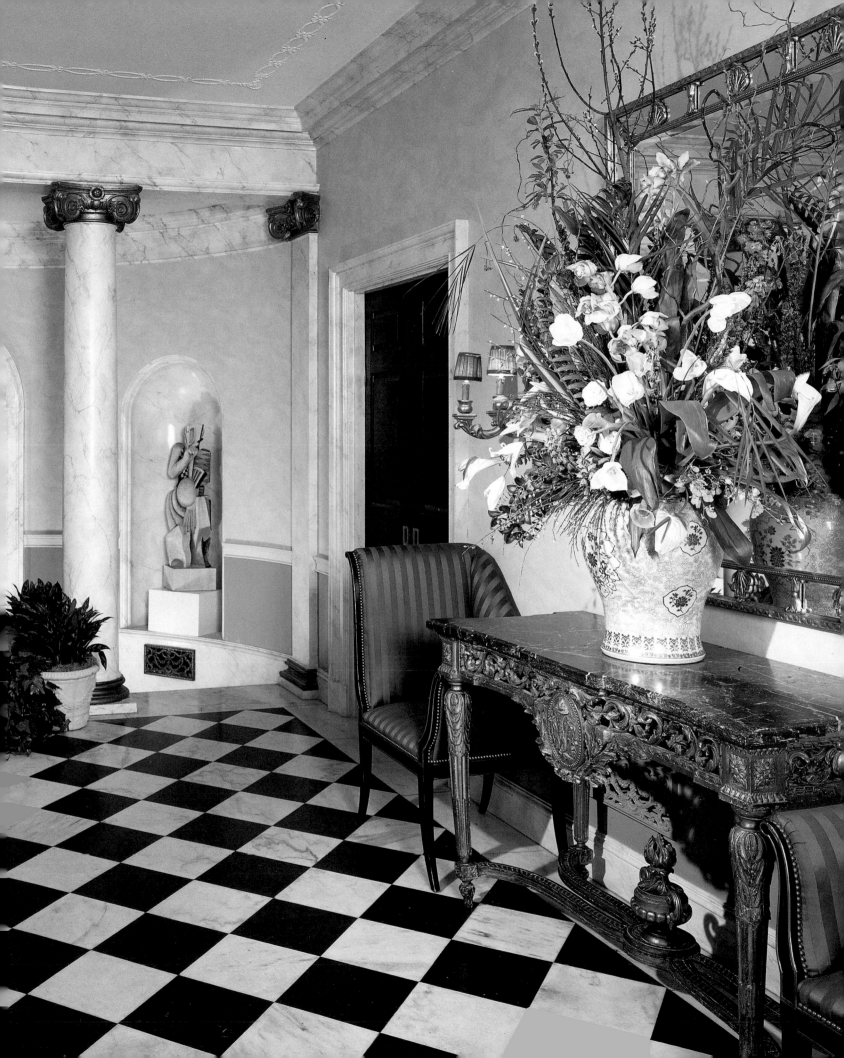

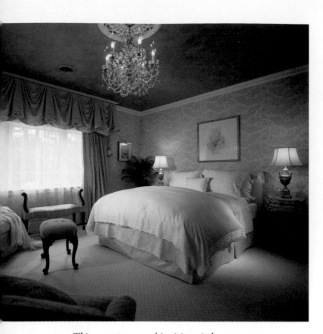

This sumptuous and inviting pied-a-terre reflects the charm and refinement of a European hotel. A serene color scheme combined with the finest linens and upholstery create a true retreat where tranquillity reigns.

Location: Atlanta, Georgia

[right] *The furnishings and accessories complement the room's grand scale and ornate architectural details.*

Location: Atlanta, Georgia

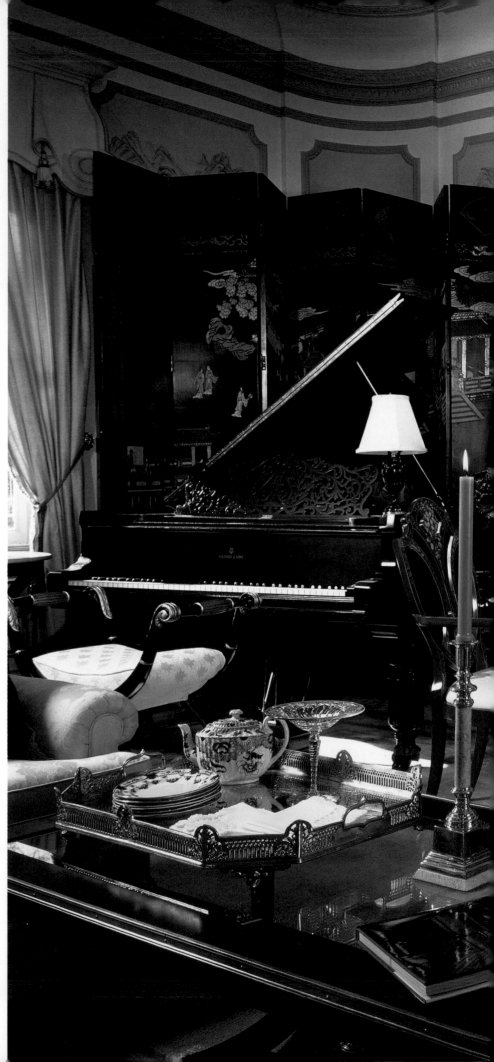

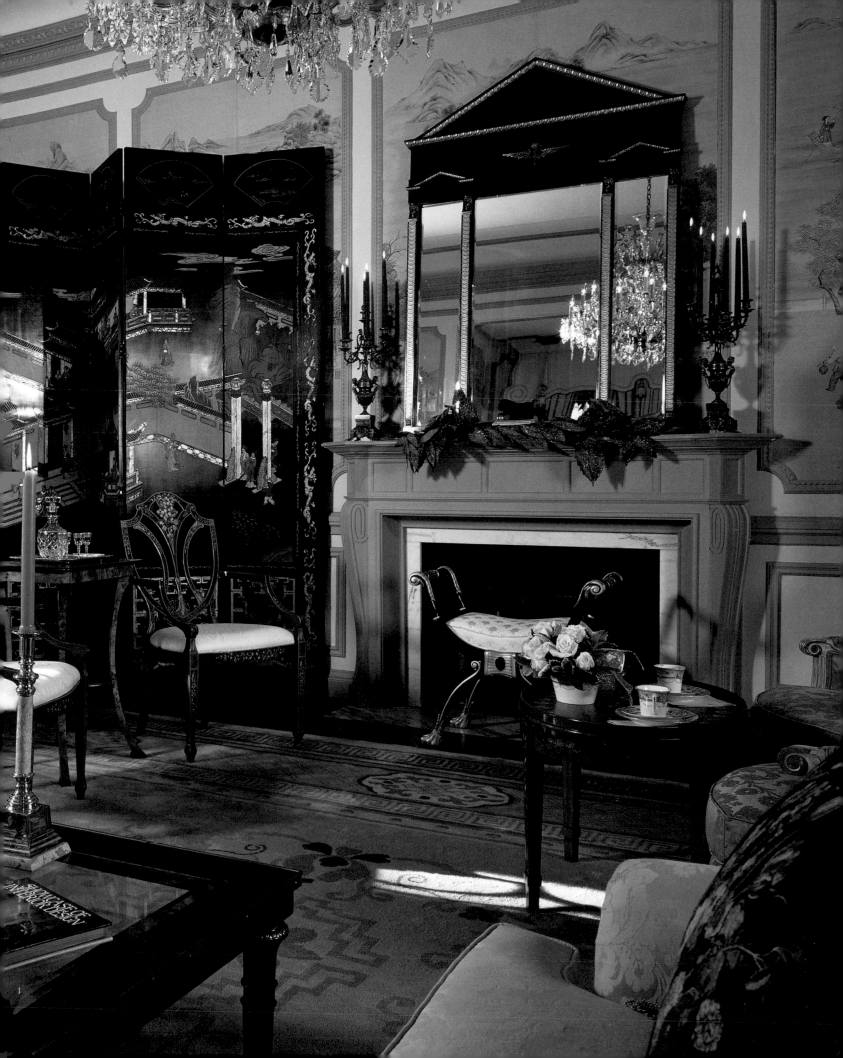

SWANN INTERIORS

With each new project, Gwen Moore Swann brings an expertise in the area of architectural design, spatial planning, lighting design, as well as the finished interior design. Her goal is to create an environment that reflects a client's lifestyle, needs, interests, and unique perspective. Through open communication, a daunting undertaking for a client can become a pleasurable and satisfying experience for finding creative solutions.

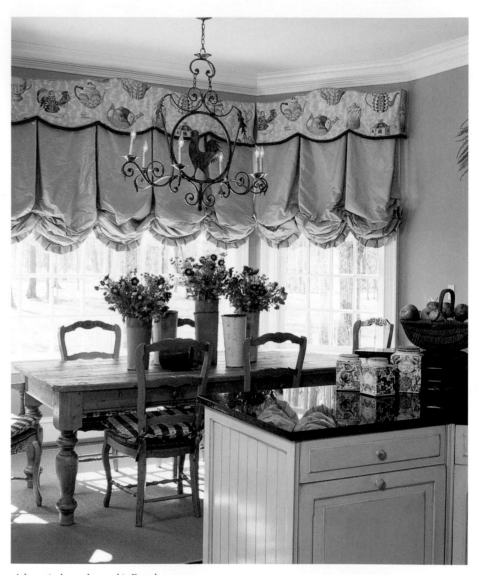

A bay window enlarges this French country kitchen and casual dining area. Rich green walls and a sophisticated window treatment imbues the space with a sensational splash of color.

Location: Macon, Georgia

[right] *The elegant foyer with its limestone and marble floor and architectural details beckons visitors into this inviting living room.*

Location: Macon, Georgia

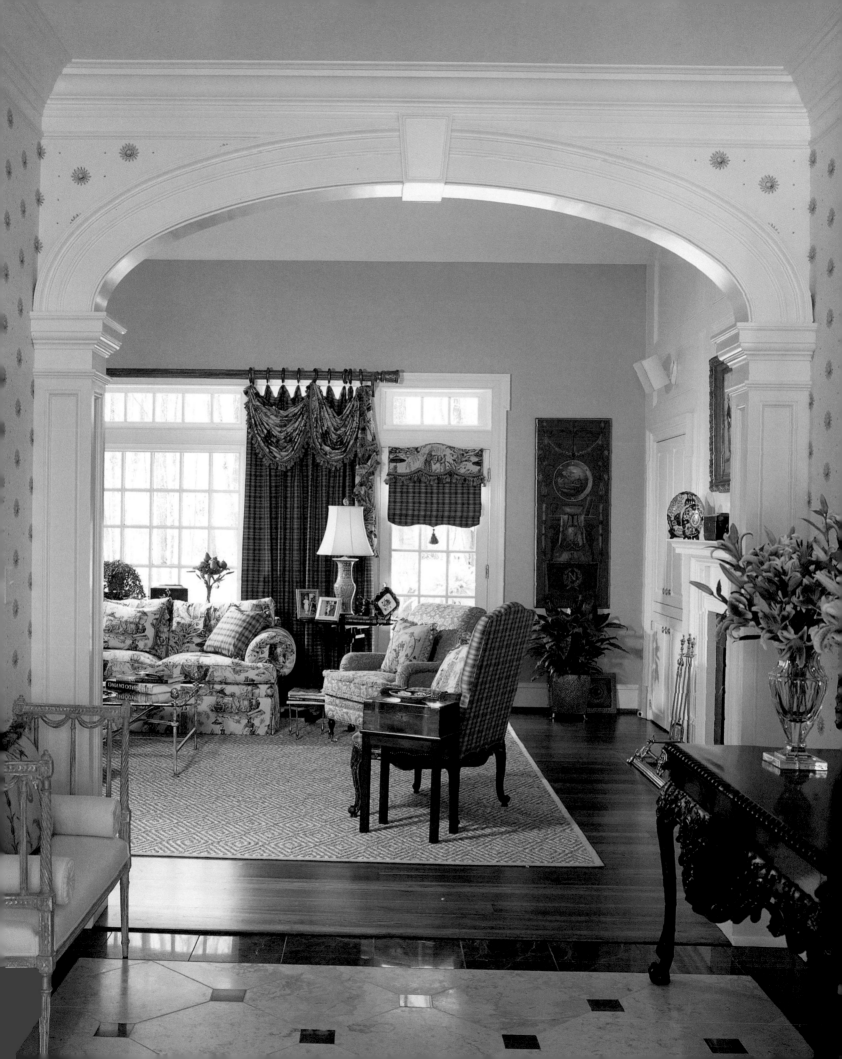

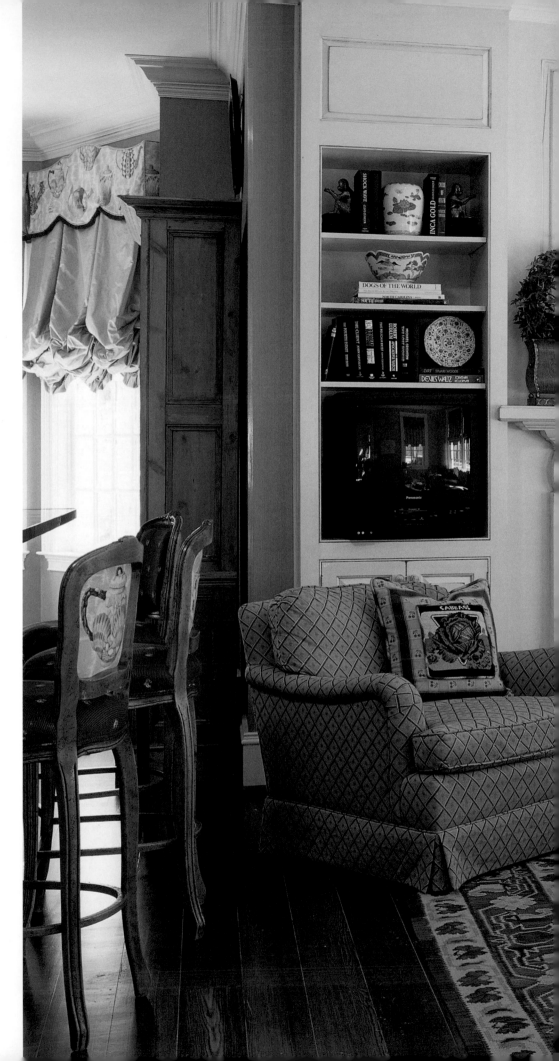

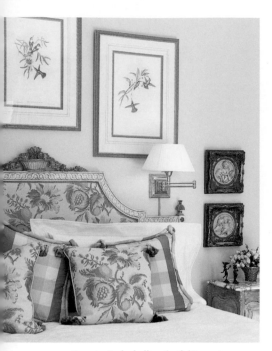

Serenity is the hallmark of this spacious and well-appointed master bedroom. The Grey Watkins tapestry instills the room with sense of charm and relaxation.

Location: Macon, Georgia

[right] *This vibrant painting by Southern artist Barbara Gallagher sets the tone for this comfortable and bright den that makes dramatic use of color and texture.*

Location: Macon, Georgia

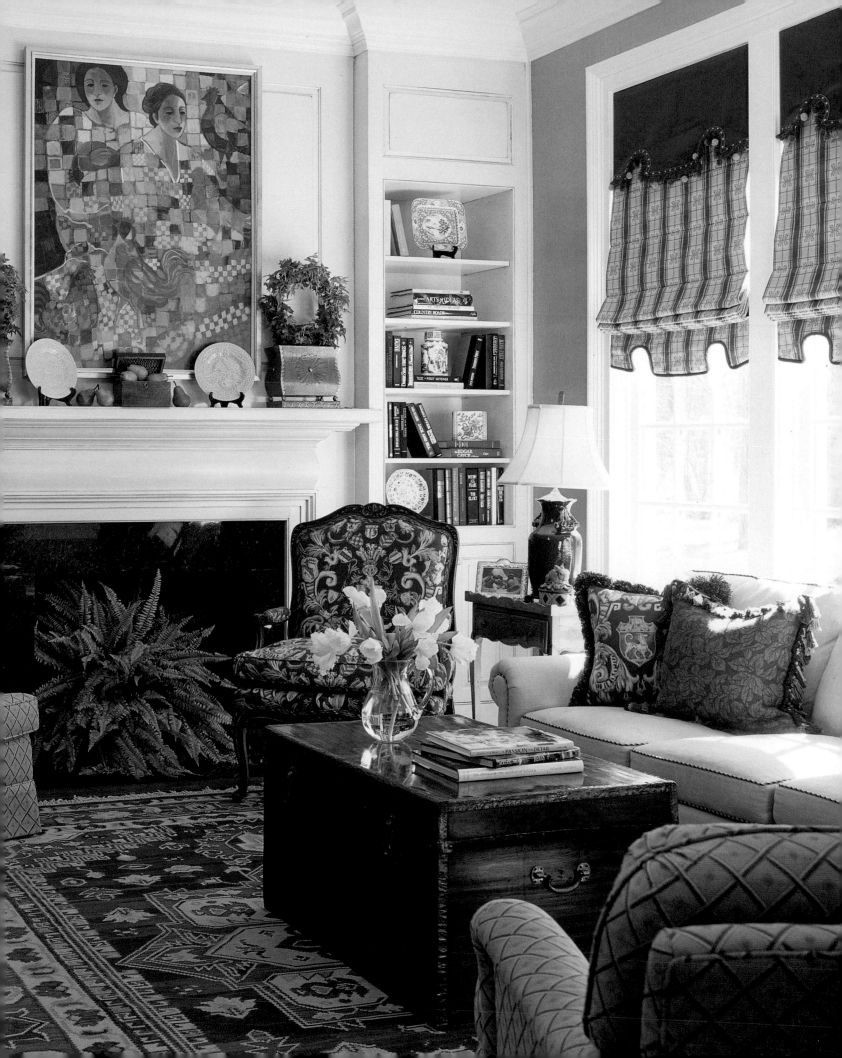

YOGGY CROW, INC.

The goal of Yoggy Crow is to create an environment that is comfortable and inviting, yet also reflects the client's taste and personality. Their combination of comfort, elegance, and individual expression make for engaging spaces that will stand the test of time.

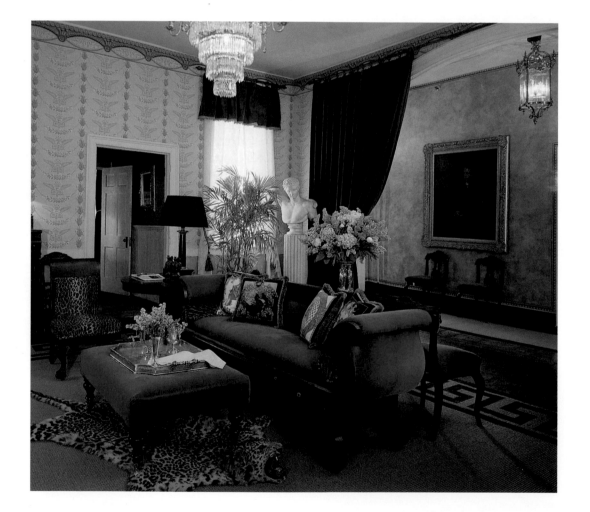

Designed to re-create the feel of the early nineteenth-century, special attention was given to the choices of fabric and wall finishes.

Location: Hanover, Virginia

[right] *Warm, rich, luxurious colors invite visitors into this recreation room at a historic tavern.*

Location: Hanover, Virginia

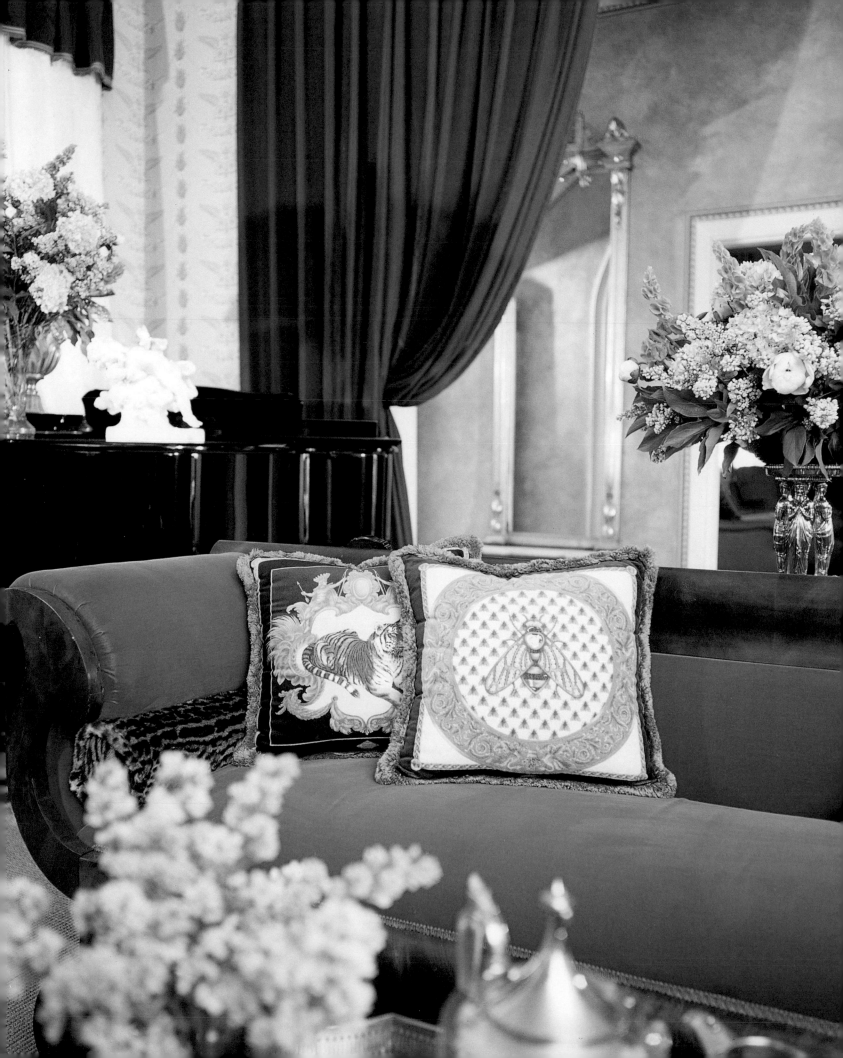

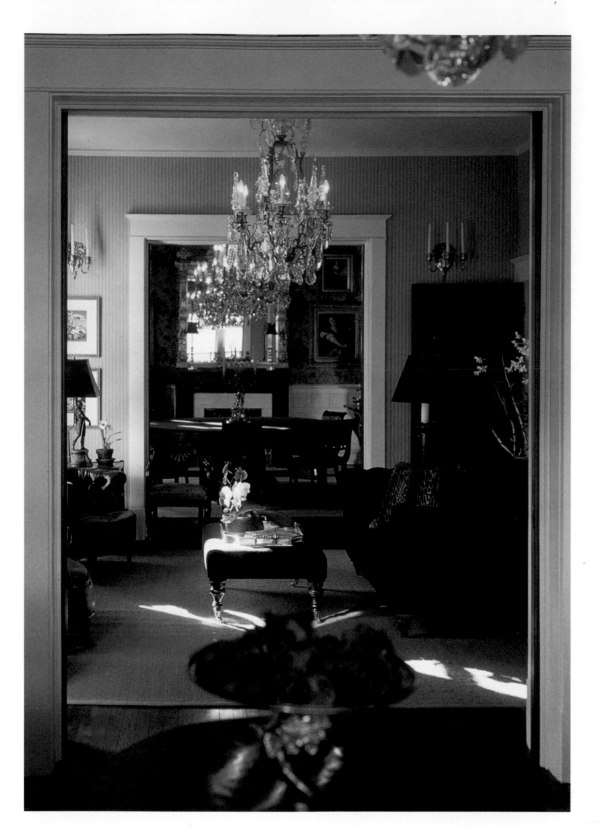

Crystal chandeliers crown these sunny rooms, which are accented with both bold and subtle stripes.

Location: Richmond, Virginia

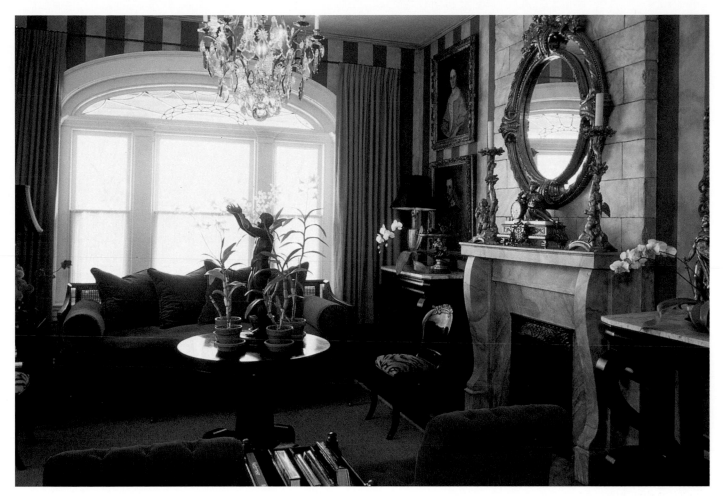

An eclectic mix of Continental
antiques lend an air of bold elegance
to this design studio's front parlor.
Faux finishes on walls and mantel-
piece add depth and texture.

Location: Richmond, Virginia

Warm color palette, soft textures, and
timeless accessories enhance a quiet
corner of this parlor.

Location: Richmond, Virginia

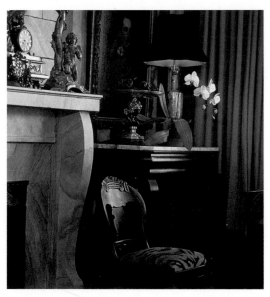

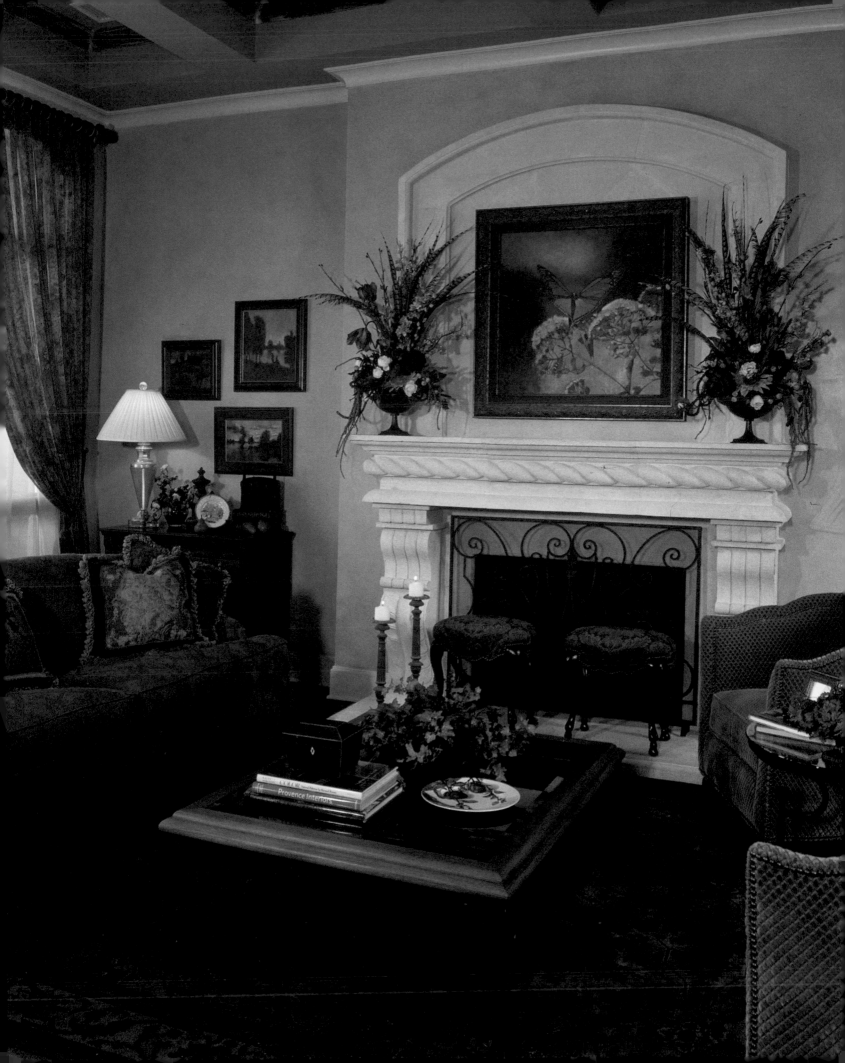

NEW SOUTH

Texas is in a class by itself. As always, it is an exception to every rule, since as a part of the New South it is also very much a part of the old frontier. The stereotype most people conjure up when they think of Texas—rough-and-tumble landscape punctuated by cactus, sturdy tin-roofed ranch houses built of hefty and durable limestone rock, wide-open spaces—is accurate, at least for the western half of the state. It is a reality that has shaped the way generations of Texans all over the state have learned to live. The stone houses typical of much of the state—quaint and appealing to city dwellers—were practical solutions to a harsh environment for their original owners. The casual plainness of the architecture; the massiveness of their walls, doors and ceiling beams; the spareness of decoration have emerged into a look that is distinctively Texan.

Today, ranch houses are back in style, and for good reason. Their wide-hanging eaves envelope a house in shady bliss on a scorching summer day;

their corrugated tin roofs handily reflect the sun's relentless rays; and their high ceilings lift the heat up and out of a room. They make life comfortable. But nowadays they have been modified to accommodate the discomfort of busy city lives. Interiors, even the most plain-spoken, are more luxurious: concrete floors are buffed, stained and waxed to a marble-like sheen; limestone countertops are polished to a satiny patina; and furniture is deeply cushioned, generously proportioned, often lavishly upholstered.

In fact, this is where the influence of the South is really felt—and not surprisingly, since at least half of the state has always been aligned with the South. Around Houston, a dark green curtain of forest rises: gone is the big Texas sky, the flat juncture of earth and sky, the sense of vastness. Huge pines, slumbering swamps massed with baroquely twined roots, branches, and vines make a lush beauty that engendered a languor more Southern than Western. When settlers from Mississippi and beyond crossed the Sabine River into East Texas and saw the streams, forests, and deep-red earth they saw land that reminded them of home. They settled there, extending the limits of the Old South. Greek revival plantations—built by lumber and rice barons—attest to its vitality. It is this volatile mix of

pioneer daring and Southern gentility that has created a look unique to the rest of the country.

In the following pages, you will see work by Texas designers. Although each has a distinctly different take on style, they all have one thing in common—total confidence in how to make a room livably beautiful. Life is active and lived full-tilt in Texas, and relaxation is taken just a seriously. Here you will see exceptional rooms for exceptional lives—roomy chairs and sofas for maximum enjoyment of time off; expansive family and living rooms for gatherings of friends from far and wide; luxurious studies and retreats for just getting away from it all. And you will see, too, that what makes the New South so new is not just its resurgent economy, but also because it firmly rests in its heritage, a wild mix of Southern and Western cultures from which the very best is drawn.

The living room combines rich architectural detailing and sumptuous furnishings for a room that is both welcoming and inspiring. Coffered ceiling, carved-stone fireplace, and large arched windows play nicely against glazed walls. Project completed in collaboration with Dawn Frank, Susie Johnson, and Kent Beardsley.

Interior Design: Linda McCalla Interiors
Location: Austin, Texas

DESIGN HOUSE

Effective design should respond to a client's lifestyle and needs, in terms of both function and aesthetics. It is important that the designer listens to and interprets the client's needs, and then works in close collaboration to create a special and unique environment. Design House offers a team approach to serve the client and to maintain close attention to detail.

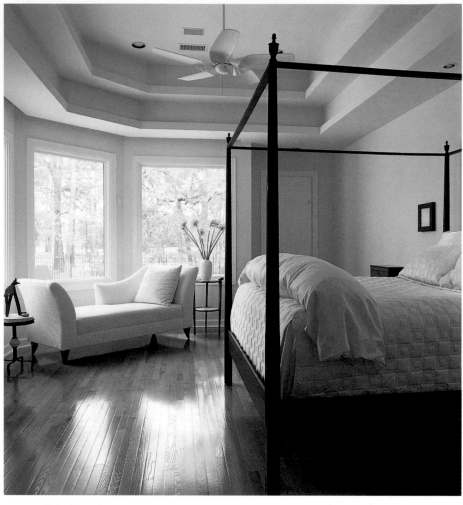

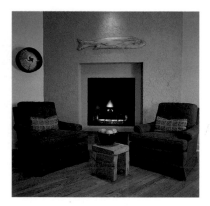

Reflecting the owner's request for a pared-down, uncluttered feeling, this family room features a tall, shallow Rumford fireplace as its focal point. Matching armchairs offer an intimate, comfortable seating in close proximity to the kitchen.

Location: The Woodlands, Texas

Motorized shades in this master bedroom completely disappear to take advantage of the view while offering privacy with a remote control. Cove lighting showcases the architectural detailing of the ceiling.

Location: The Woodlands, Texas

[right] *Eighteen-foot-tall ceilings of the living room instill a sense of drama. The curved-glass railing enhances the space's sense of openness. Tall windows offer striking views to the pool and outdoor firepit. Honed marble floors offer a layer of texture and elegance.*

Location: The Woodlands, Texas

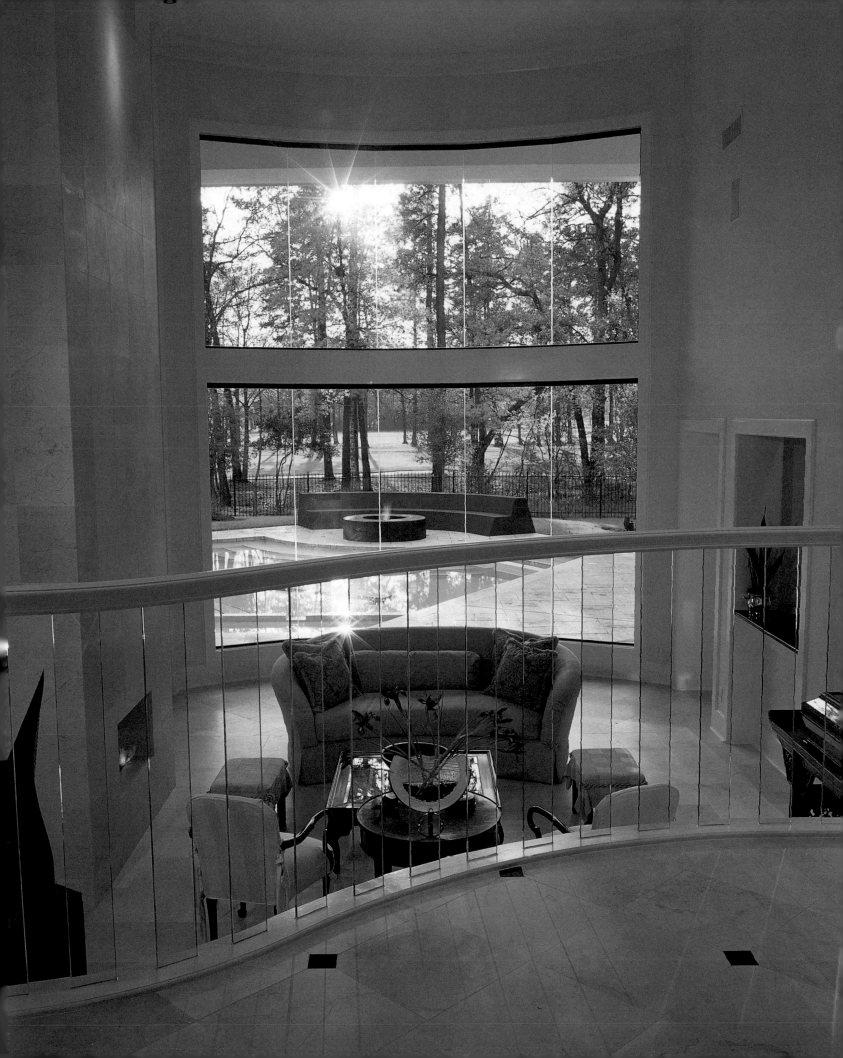

JANE PAGE CREATIVE DESIGNS

With an affinity for richness in form and finishes, Jane Page-Crump always assesses the dramatic and aesthetic to create designs that complement and enhance quality architecture. The firm provides clients with functional, comfortable, and timeless designs through an artistic balancing of color, textures, and patterns. A full-service design firm, Jane Page Creative Designs specializes in new construction, providing creative design advice on custom cabinets, architectural details, natural materials, and distinctive finishes.

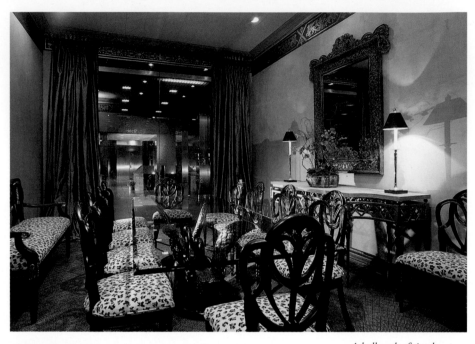

A hallmark of timeless design, this corporate conference room with its engaging blending of rich color, varied textures, and refined finishes conveys a look of traditional stability.

Location: Houston, Texas

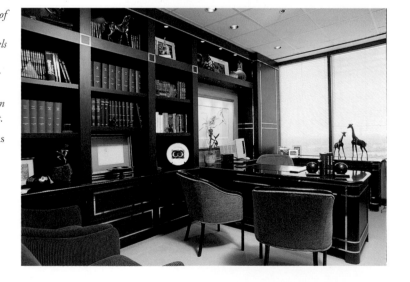

Custom cabinetry crafted of mahogany and accented with brass insets and panels of tambour enlivens this commercial office. Surface and storage requirements were met while creating an elegant work environment.

Location: Houston, Texas

[right] *A balance of soft colors, interesting textures, and sophisticated furnishings establishes understated beauty in this Houston showhouse.*

Location: Houston, Texas

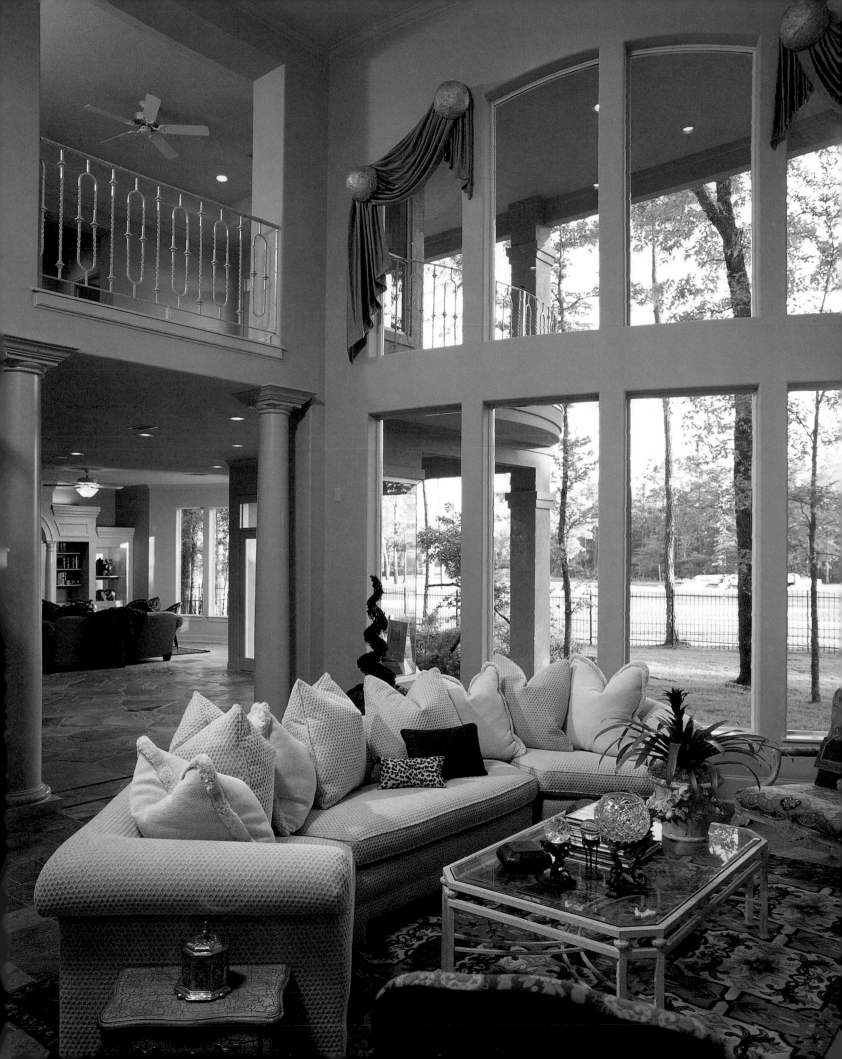

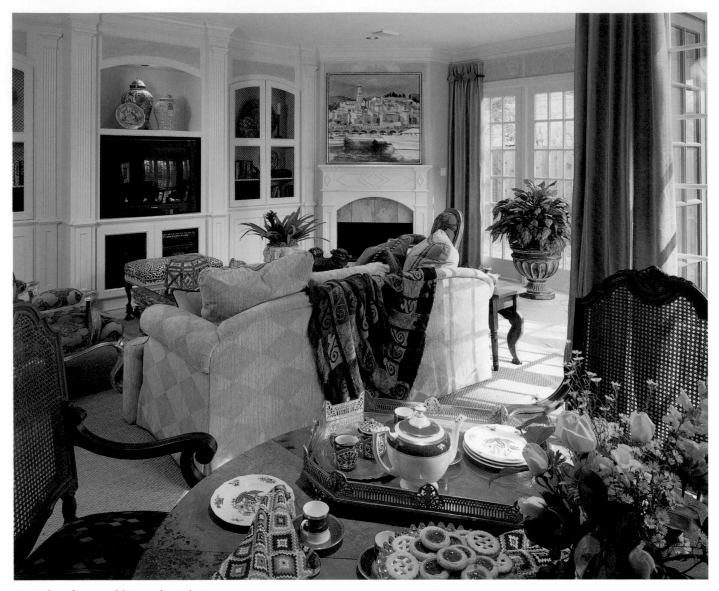

A mingling of textures, fabrics, and period pieces imbues this room with comfort and sophistication. Antique chairs with their natural finish sit comfortably around a custom-designed slate and iron table. Stylized Louis XV chairs with an aged silver finish complement the room's intimate seating arrangement.

Location: Houston, Texas

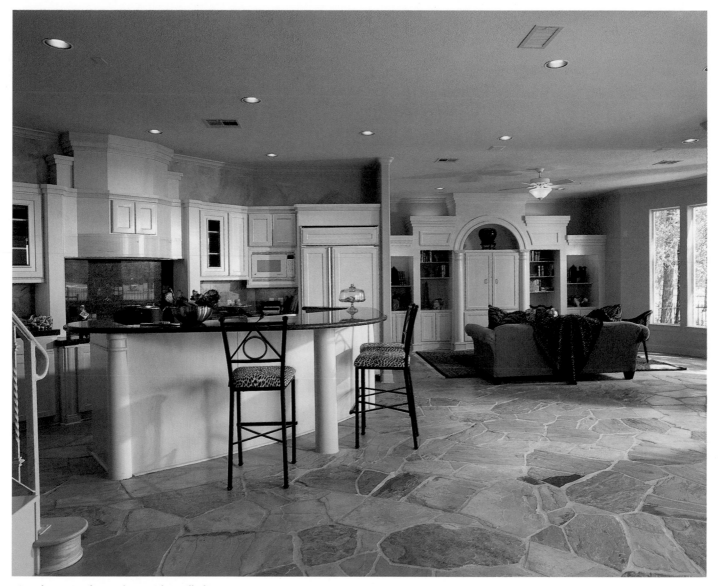

An urbane mix of natural materials instills this kitchen and adjacent sitting area with character and drama. Architectural detailing enlivens custom cabinets; granite counters and a slate floor add layers of texture and warmth.

Location: Houston, Texas

LINDA McCALLA INTERIORS

Located in historic downtown Georgetown, Texas, Linda McCalla Interiors is a full-service interior design firm. Offering three registered interior designers who concentrate primarily on residential projects in the central-Texas region, the firm has been commissioned for projects in Philadelphia and Washington, D.C. The firm creates interiors reflecting both the architectural style of the structure and the unique taste of the client. Architectural detailing, rich material finishes, and a sophisticated mix of furnishings combine to create stylish yet relaxed interiors.

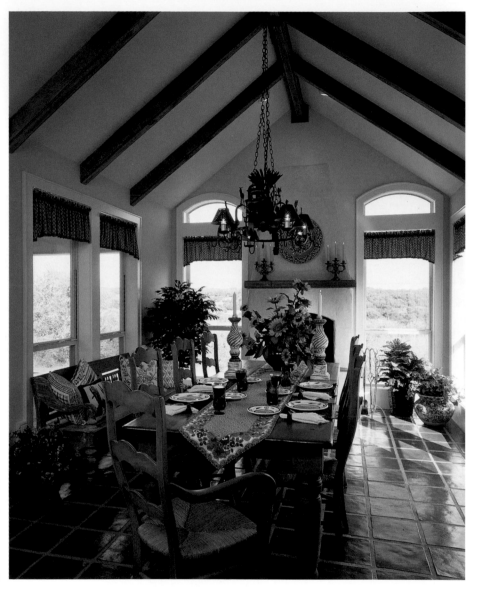

A large pine table and French ladderback chairs make a grand statement in this dining room. Colorful Italian pottery adorns the raised, hooded fireplace while country French fabrics frame the dramatic Hill Country view.

Location: Georgetown, Texas

[right] *Casual elegance reflecting the distinct Texas Hill Country style was the inspiration for this living room. Overstuffed upholstery combined with primitive antiques enhance the room's dramatic architectural elements.*

Location: Georgetown, Texas

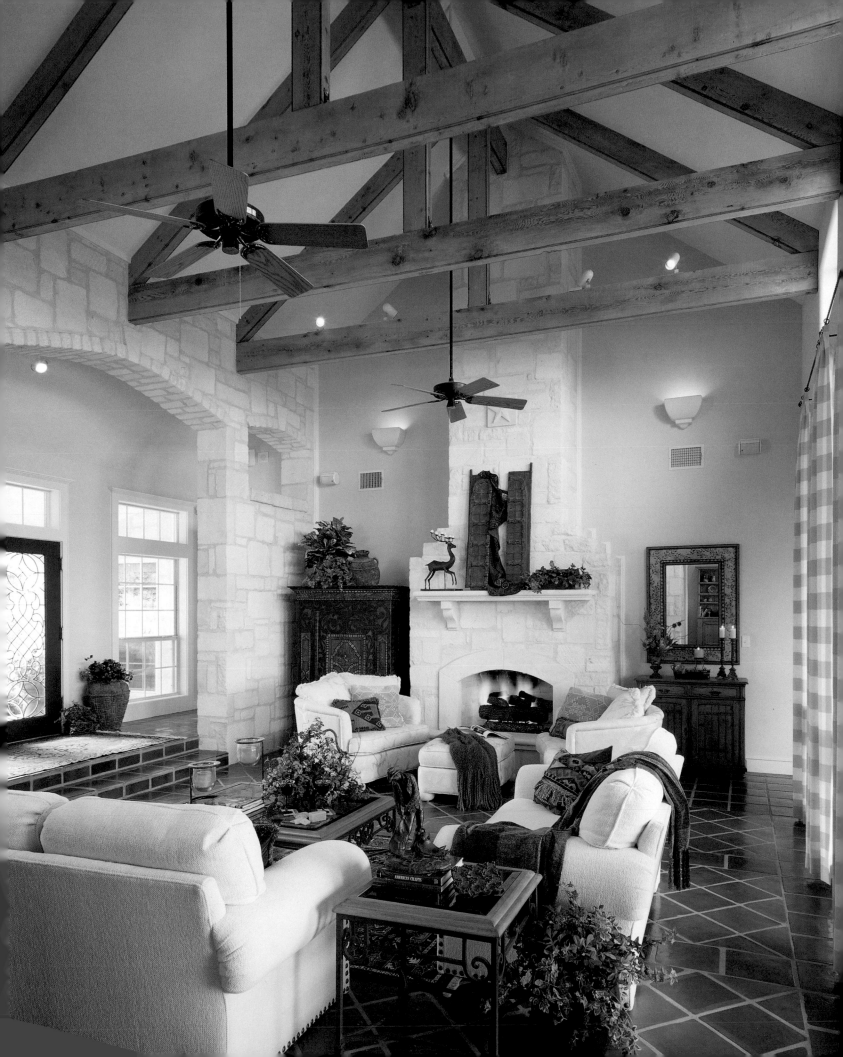

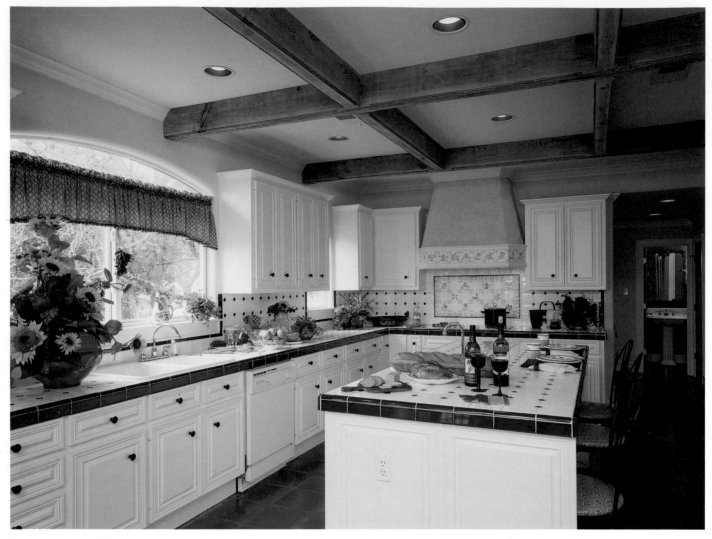

Rough cedar beams define the ceiling while crisp, white cabinetry and blue-and-white tiles are handsomely contrasted to creamy walls and Saltillo tile floors. Hand-painted tiles decorate the hooded stove.

Location: Georgetown, Texas

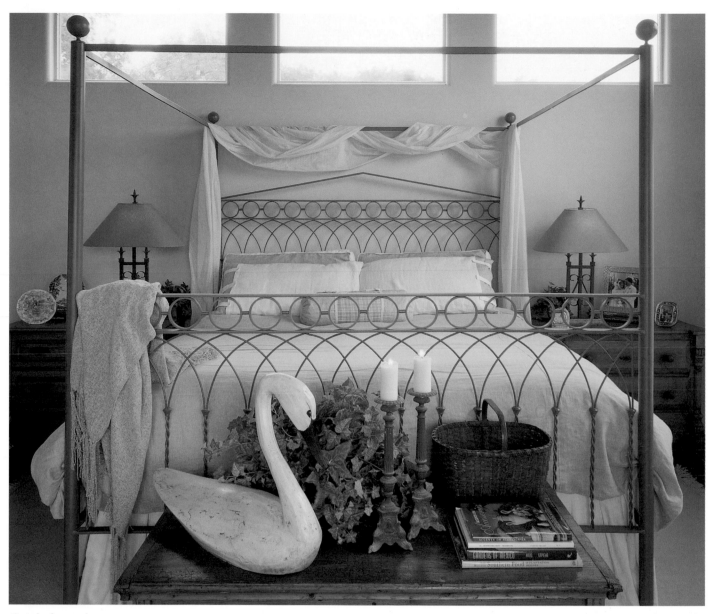

*Quietly elegant, the master
bedroom features a classically
detailed iron bed layered with
linen. Pine chests, a Berber
rug, and a simple gathering of
accessories complete the look.*

Location: Georgetown, Texas

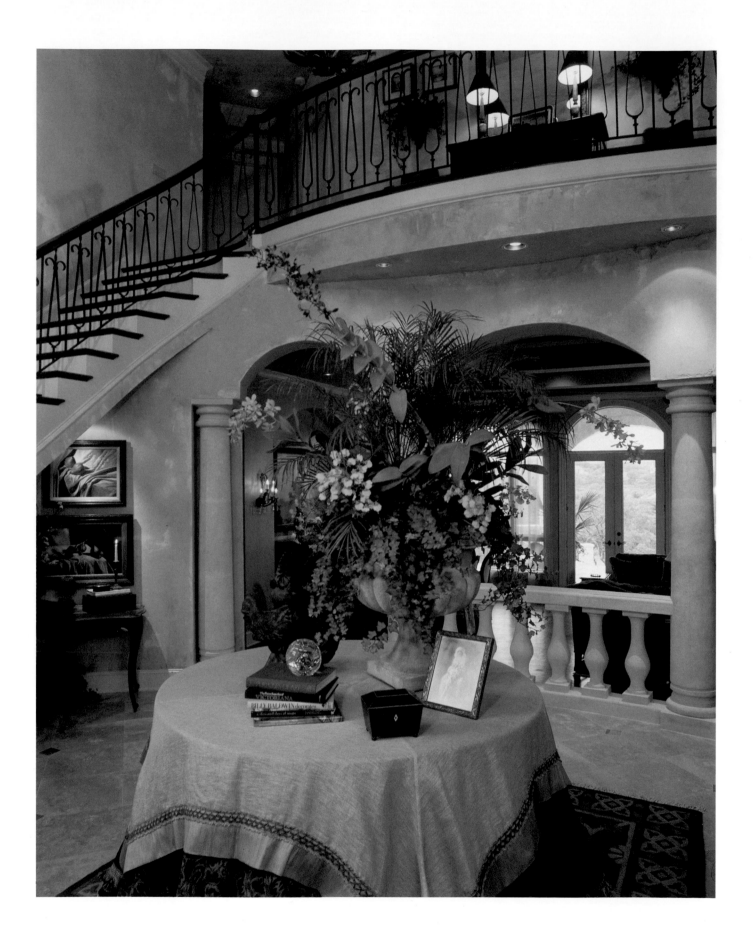

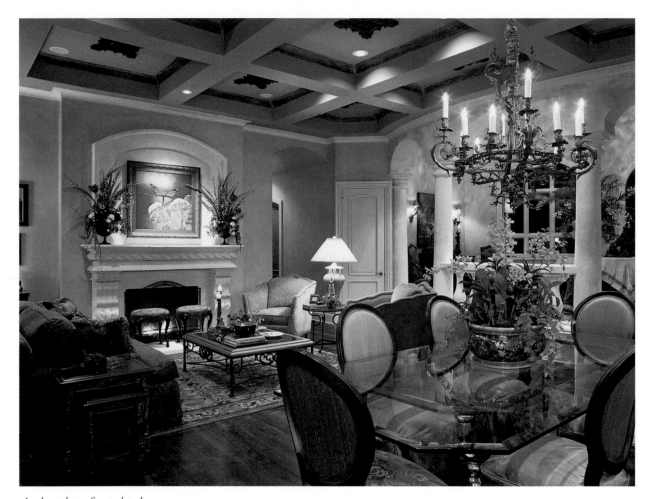

A color palette of muted amber and moss tones creates an inviting interchange between the living and dining areas. The architectural details establish a rich backdrop for antiques, art, and a distinctive rug. Project completed in collaboration with Dawn Frank, Susie Johnson, and Kent Beardsley.

Location: Austin, Texas

[left] *Inspired by European country architecture, the entry features elegantly simple elements executed on a grand scale. Sweeping staircase, stone columns and balustrade, and ornamental iron dramatically punctuate the frescoed walls. A luxuriously draped table, French antiques and fine art enhance the architecture. Project completed in collaboration with Dawn Frank, Susie Johnson, and Kent Beardsley.*

Location: Austin, Texas

The living room combines rich architectural detailing and sumptuous furnishings for a room that is both welcoming and inspiring. Coffered ceiling, carved-stone fireplace, and large arched windows play nicely against glazed walls. Project completed in collaboration with Dawn Frank, Susie Johnson, and Kent Beardsley.

Location: Austin, Texas

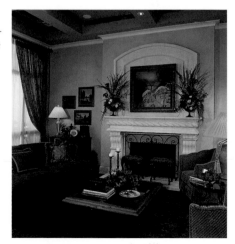

MYRL TALKINGTON DESIGNS

Working in many formats ranging from ethnic to seventeenth-century English motif, the Talkington firm employs a wide variety of tastes and styles. Their philosophy is to listen carefully to their clients so that each installation will reflect the client's own personality. Many questions are asked and many hours are spent looking at the client's own treasures, from travel acquisitions to family heirlooms. Implementing the philosophy of blending the client's personal touches with the best of today's furnishings and fabrics is a time-consuming endeavor and an ever new challenge for the firm.

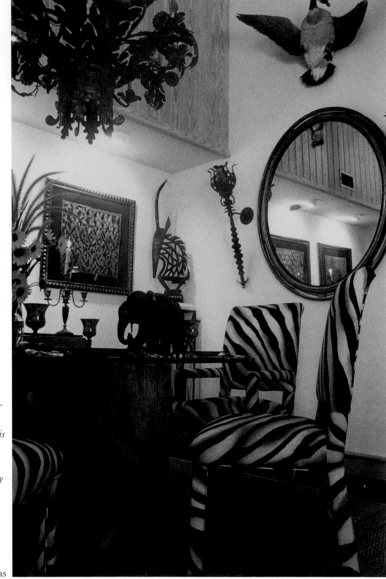

Intended as a weekend retreat, this home employs a combination of native-African and classic European motifs that were common in the early part of this century in both South Africa and Kenya. The dining room features Kuba cloths collected by the client on African travels combined with an eigthteenth-century French mirror and antique French cypress table base.

Location: Lake Whitney, Texas

[right] *The baby grand Steinway is a welcome addition for frequent entertaining in this engaging garden room. Bold colors and striking accessories including a nineteenth-century Sarouk rug and English writing desk accentuate the rather small space.*

Location: Dallas, Texas

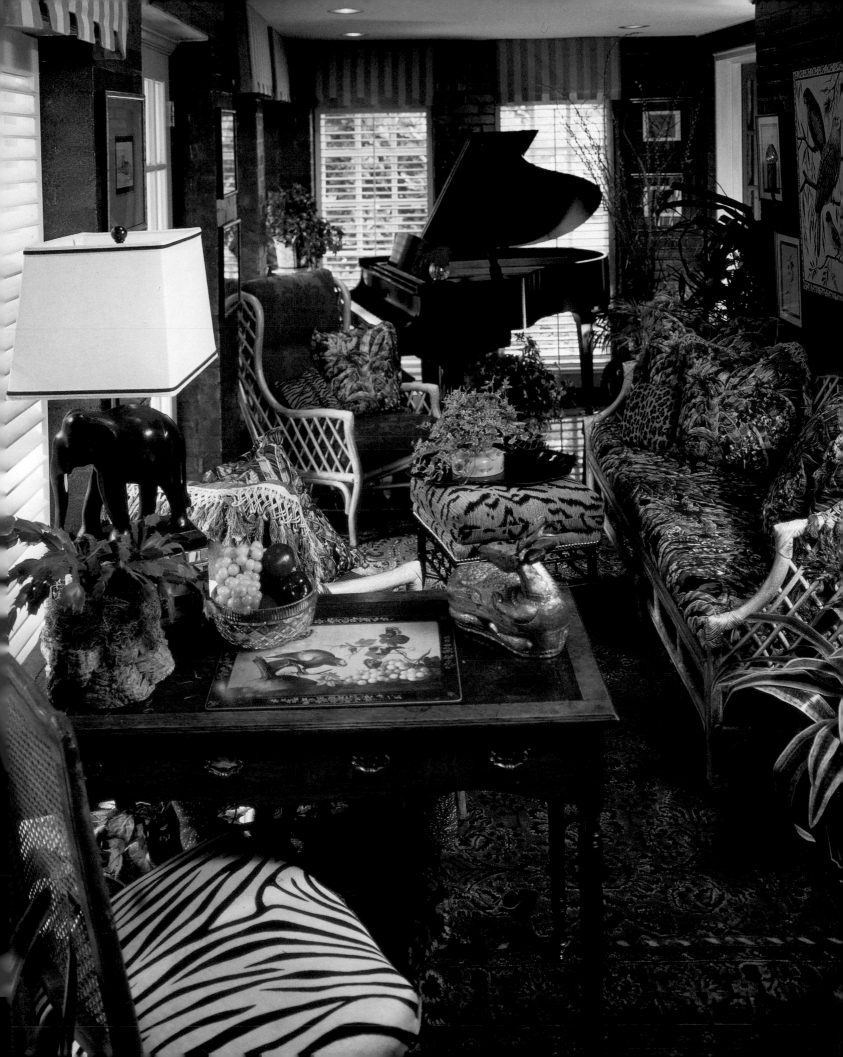

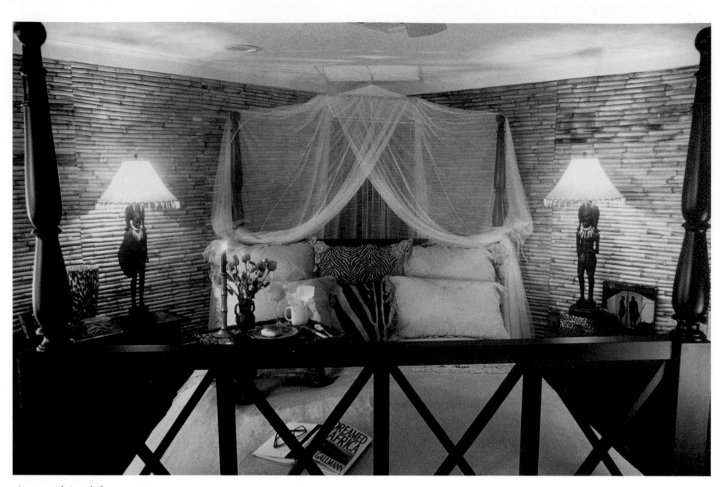

A custom-designed, four-poster bed draped with mosquito cloth and spreads of Irish linen enlivens the bedroom. Bamboo wall coverings create the perfect backdrop for the Moroccan chest purchased by the client's wife.

Location: Lake Whitney, Texas

[right] *Symmetry instills this arrangement with classical formality. An eighteenth-century French mirror serves as a dramatic focal point.*

Location: Dallas, Texas

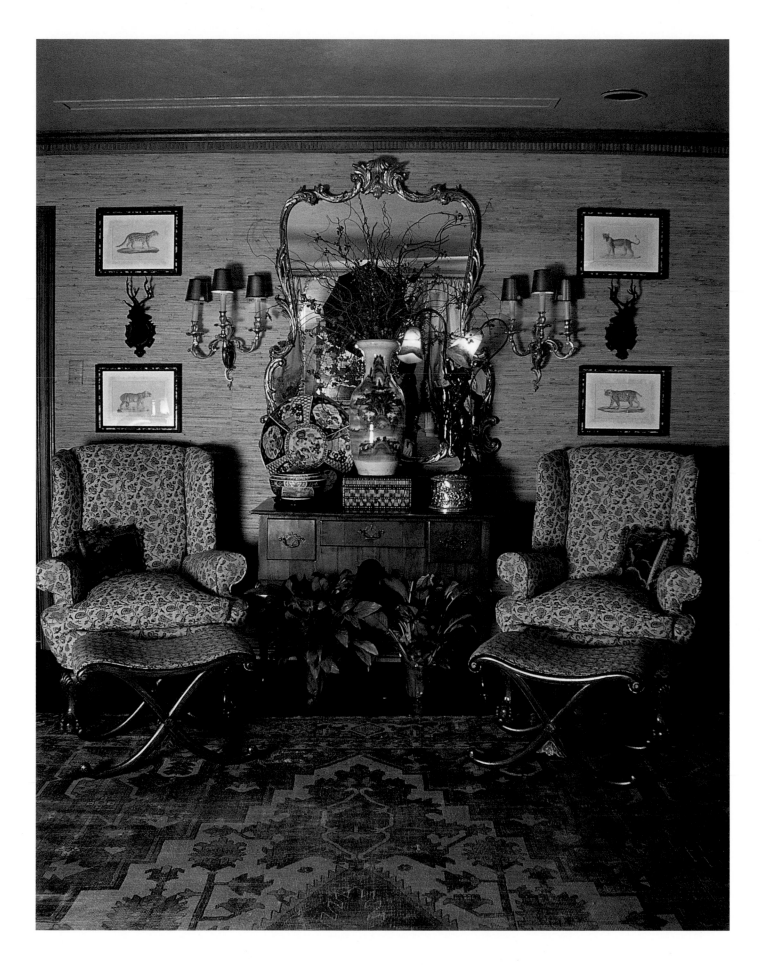

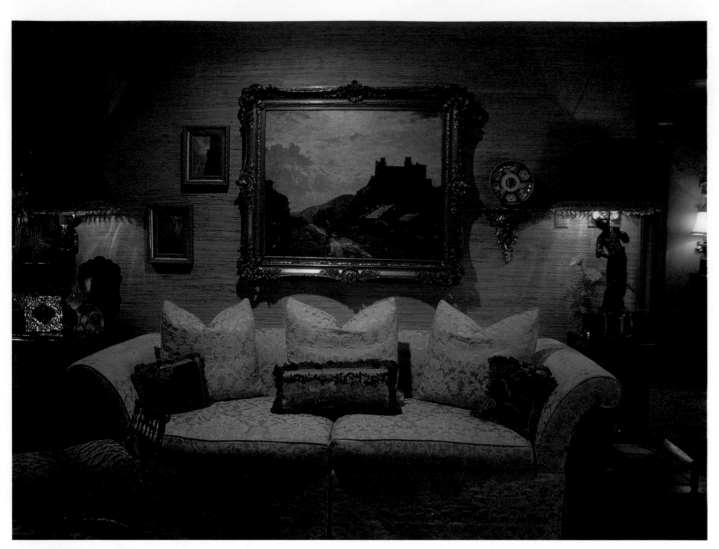

A pair of Nubian lamps frame either side of an antique Irish oil painting from the client's own collection to create an elegant sitting room. Seventeenth-century French tapestry pillows adorn the sofa. The classic Jacobean chair features its original tapestry.

Location: Dallas, Texas

A masterful mix of furnishings, art, and accessories imbue this space with drama. The best of today's fabrics and furniture are blended with collections from the client's travels to create a sophisticated look, including a seventeenth-century Chinese screen.

Location: Dallas, Texas

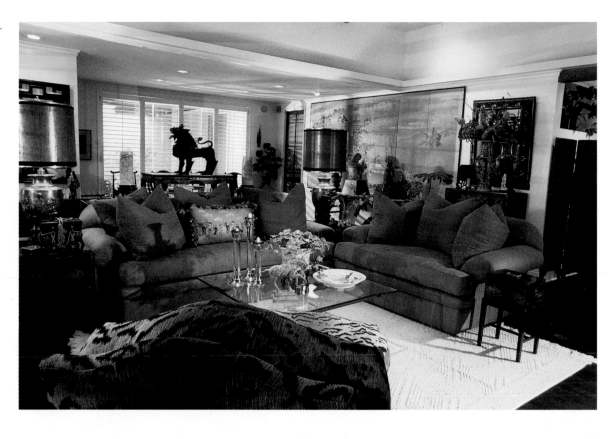

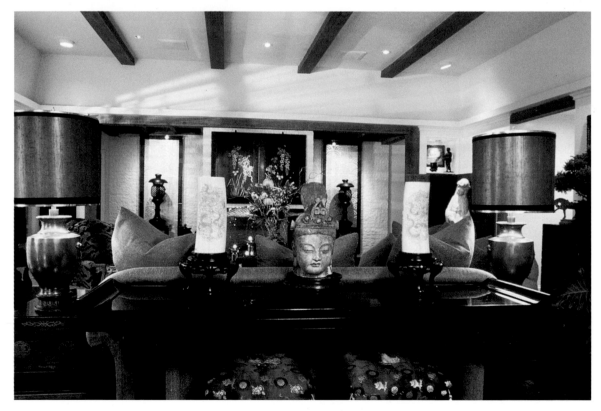

ROGERS-FORD L.C., ARCHITECTURE INTERIOR DESIGN

Nancy Rogers, a registered interior designer, and Patrick Ford, a registered architect, formed Rogers-Ford in 1990 after working together at other design firms for more than five years. The firm comprises ten talented architects and interior designers. Their unique partnership allows the firm to produce seamless designs—providing complete architectural and interior design services or working separately for clients depending upon their needs.

The firm believes the best works of architecture and interior design are not style specific, and their diverse collection of projects ranges from rustic mountain retreats to sophisticated Mediterranean-inspired residences. Their goal is to create unique spaces tailored around the individual client's personality and lifestyle. This is achieved through the incorporation of distinctive architectural details and artistically designed furnishings, fixtures, and accessories.

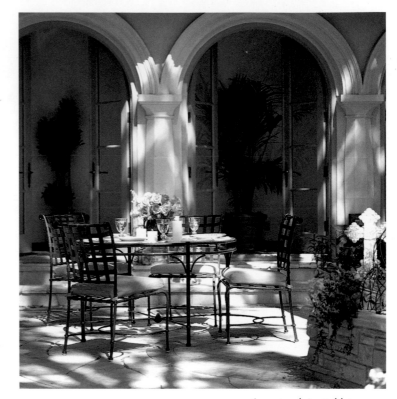

A courtyard situated between the formal living room and dining rooms, flanked by an arched gallery, extends the entertainment space of this Mediterranean home to the outdoors.

Location: Dallas, Texas

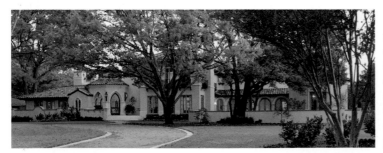

This Mediterranean home was designed to ramble among existing, mature trees on a large lot. Although new, the house has a feeling of permanence that blends with its more established neighbors.

Location: Dallas, Texas

[right] An antique Bessarabian rug on a limestone floor combine with a cypress and poplar paneled ceiling and richly textured fabrics create Old World charm in this living room.

Location: Dallas, Texas

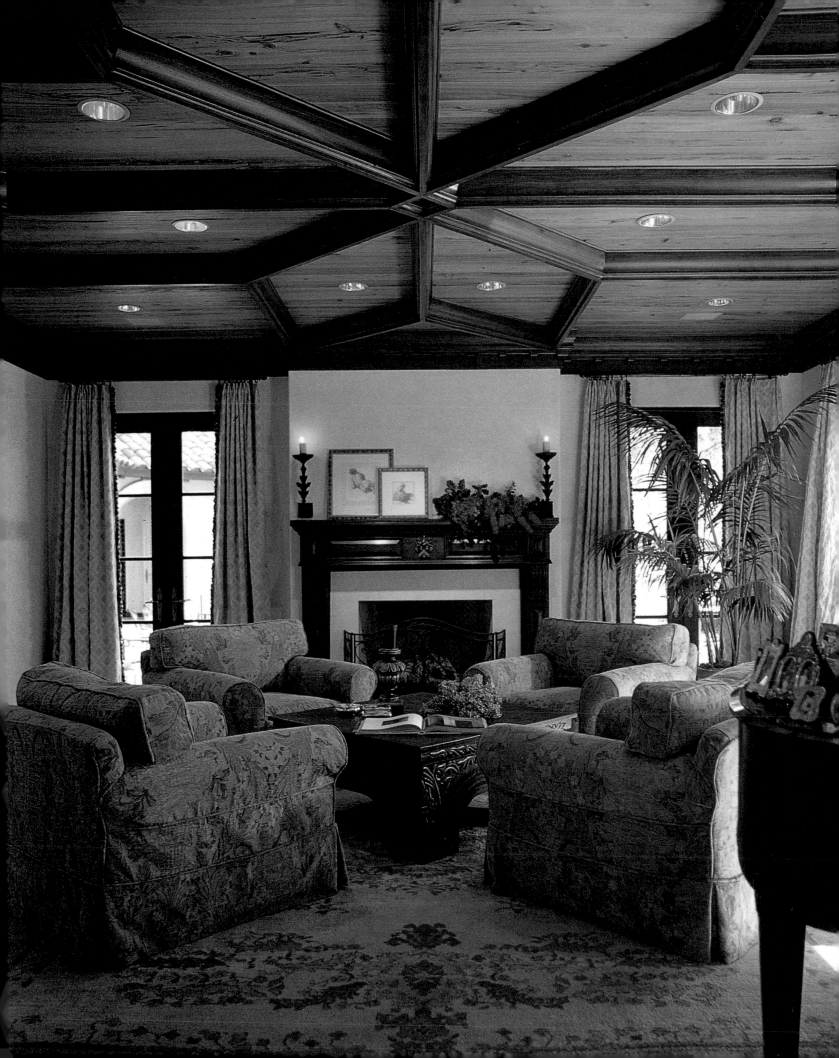

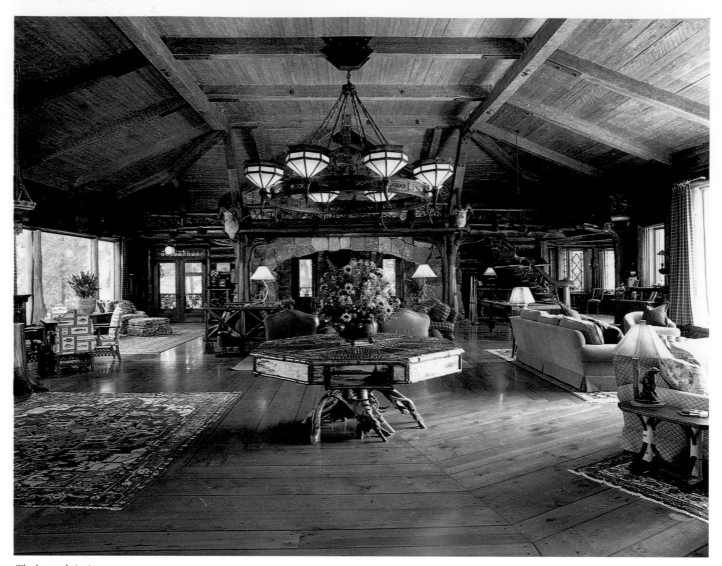

The key to designing any room is the proper use of scale. The intelligent and artistic use of furniture and decorative details brings this great room in a historic Adirondack lodge into focus.

Location: Paul Smiths, New York

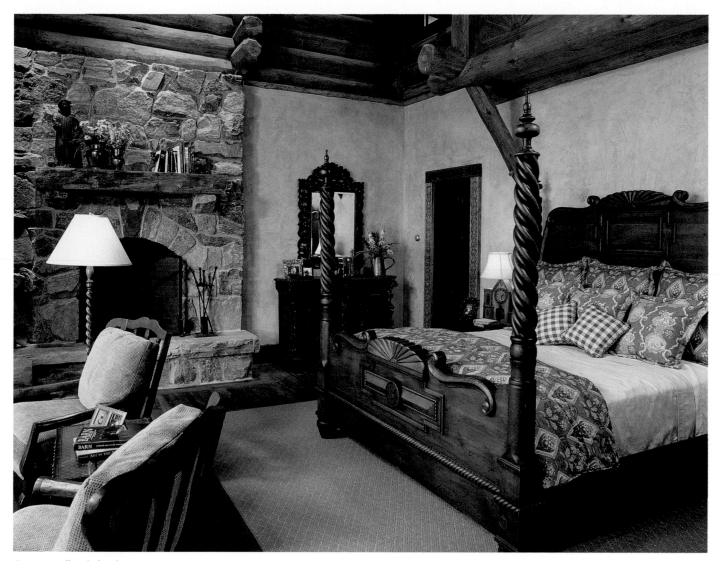

Intricate millwork details and deeply carved furnishings, including an antique sideboard and mirror and a handcrafted bed, convey Germanic themes that inspired this Adirondack cabin.

Location: Paul Smiths, New York

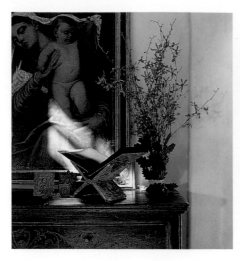

The artistry is in the details in the foyer composition. The combination of a cherished oil painting and a seventeenth-century Venetian coffer individualizes this space and beckons guests to the European home.

Location: Dallas, Texas

Arched shutters, dark wood beams, and an Italian bed instill this guest room with a sense of European character and charm.

Location: Dallas, Texas

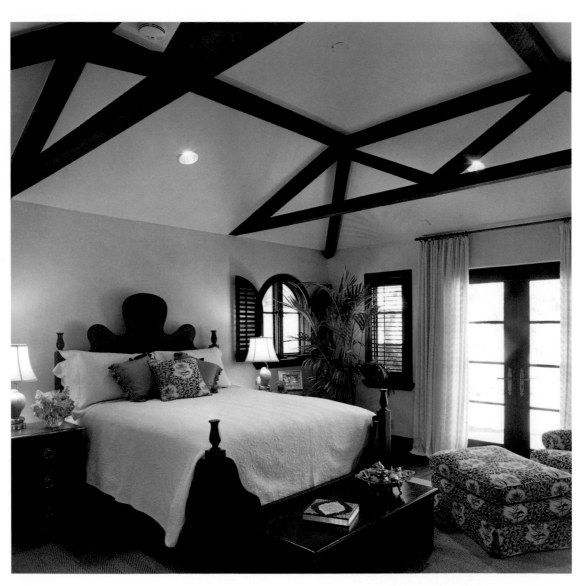

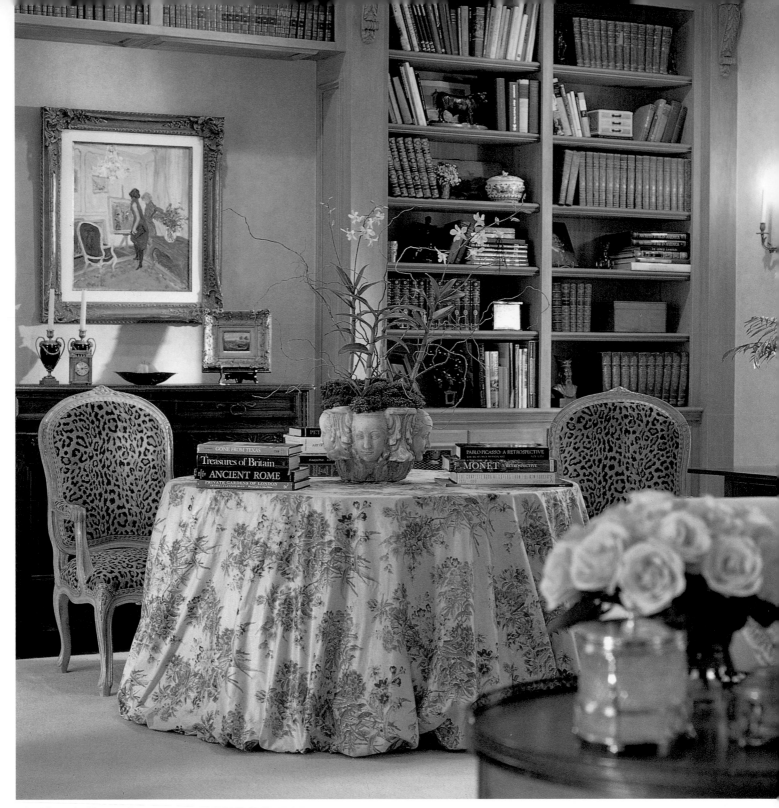

This library doubles as a dining room. The table drape can be removed and table leaves added to accommodate a large dinner party, while retaining the room's intimate setting.

Location: Dallas, Texas

CHERYL A. VAN DUYNE, ASID, INTERIOR DESIGNER

As an independent interior designer, Cheryl A. Van Duyne visualizes and achieves finished spaces that meet her clients' goals and expectations. Diversity of style is the hallmark of her design service business. She welcomes the challenge of producing unique designs regardless of client preference in style. Her greatest reward is achieving a client's design goals and thereby making their lives more enjoyable. In addition to providing interior design services, Van Duyne frequently executes an entire project through her trade and artisan resources. She holds to the philosophy that successful project execution is possible only through excellent teamwork, and builds the team by establishing trust and mutual respect between herself and the trades involved in each project. Her desire for perfection is the reason she prefers to work independently, which allows direct participation, and therefore, better control of each project.

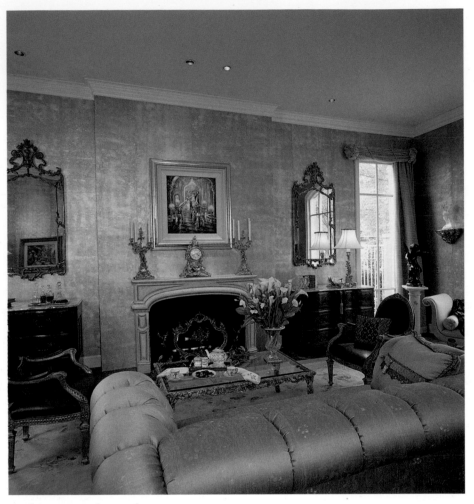

An elegant space to showcase the client's art and beautiful furnishings was the main objective. The comfortable sofa and chairs invite long conversations and afternoon teas.

Location: Dallas, Texas

[right] *The subtle color scheme allows outside color and light to dominate this conservatory. The result is an open, cheerful space that gives the feeling of actually being outside.*

Location: Dallas, Texas

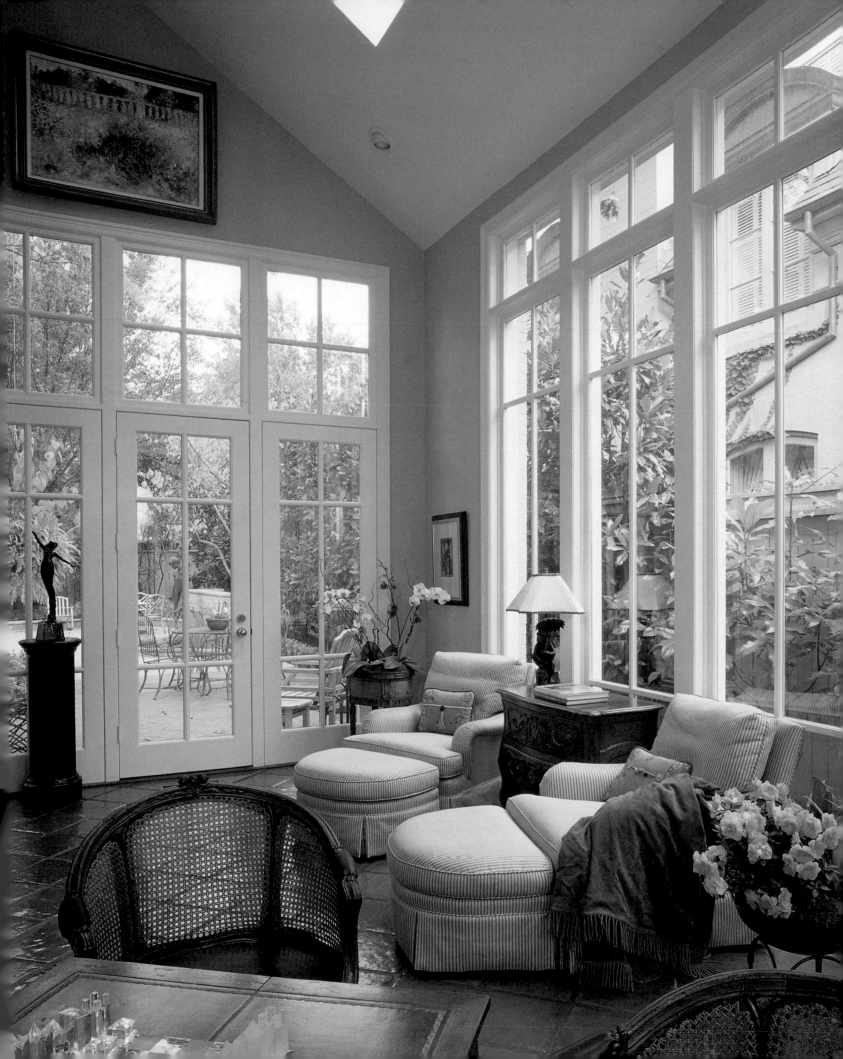

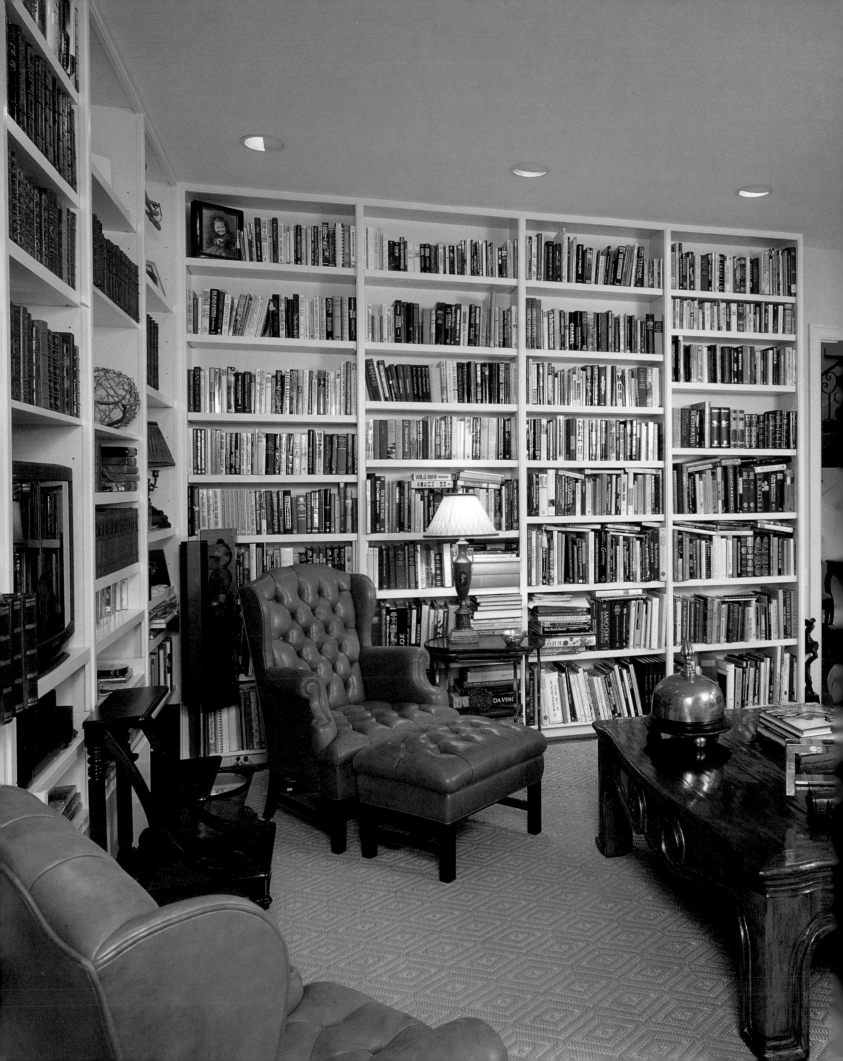

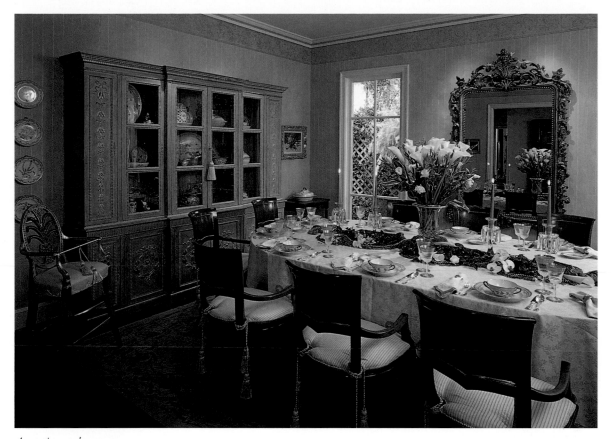

An antique aubusson rug, wallcoverings, and fabrics with soft metallic finishes provide an elegant background for the exquisite collection of china, crystal and flatware. Armchairs encourage after-dinner conversation and comfort.

Location: Dallas, Texas

Before remodeling, this entrance was dark and lacked architectural interest. The existing entrance had a solid-wood panel door. The new door and sidelights complement the existing architecture, let in lots of light, and make a beautiful entry.

Location: Dallas, Texas

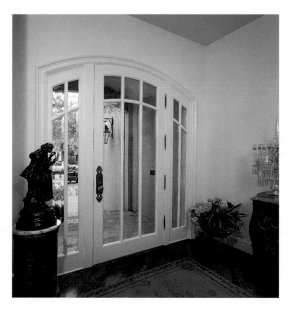

[left] *Comfortable seating, a hand-woven rug, unusual accessories, and lots of books add up to a pleasant library for reading and relaxing.*

Location: Dallas, Texas

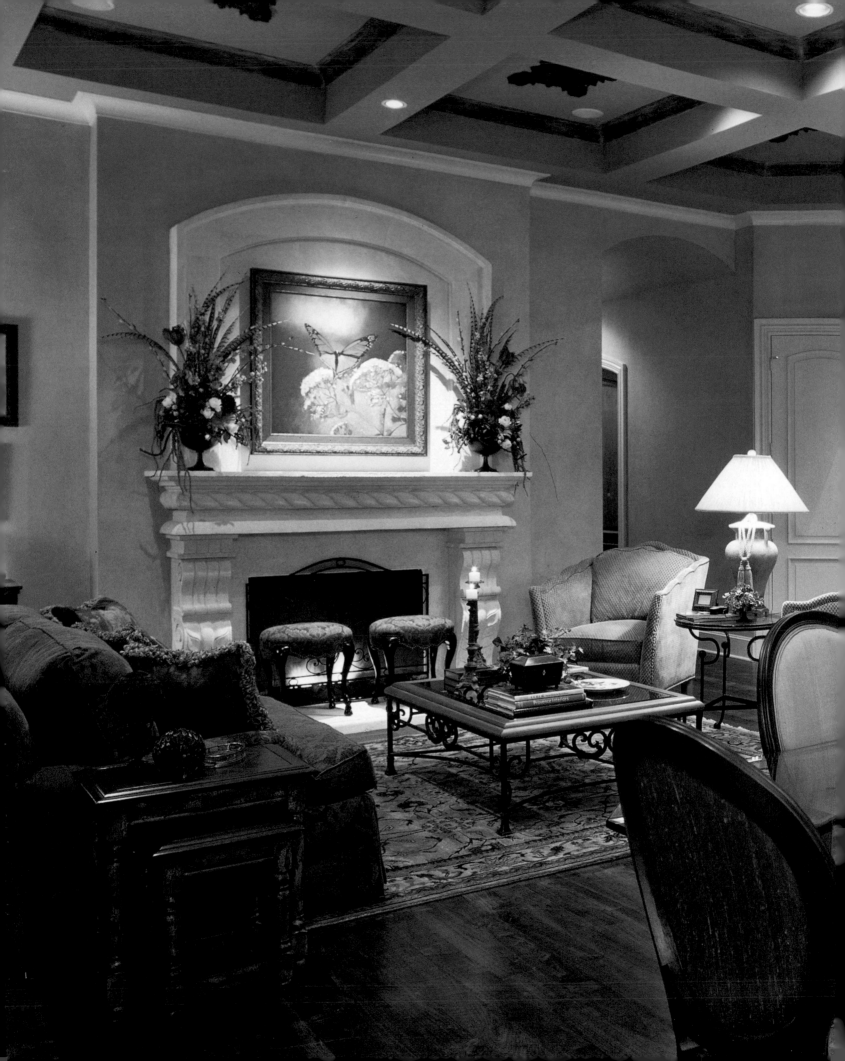

PHOTOGRAPHY CREDITS

COASTAL SOUTH

page:

8 Laurence F. Taylor
9 Laurence F. Taylor
10 Laurence F. Taylor
11 Laurence F. Taylor
14 Dennis Krukowski
15 Dennis Krukowski
16 Dennis Krukowski
17 Dennis Krukowski
18 Dennis Krukowski
19 Dennis Krukowski
26 Dennis Krukowski
27 Dennis Krukowski
28 Jack Gardner
29 Jack Gardner
30 Jack Gardner
31 Jack Gardner
32 Jack Gardner
33 Jack Gardner
34 Sargent Architectural Photography
35 Sargent Architectural Photography
36 Sargent Architectural Photography
37 Sargent Architectural Photography
38 Sargent Architectural Photography
39 Sargent Architectural Photography
40 Peter Margonelli
41 Peter Margonelli
42 Peter Margonelli
43 Peter Margonelli
44 Greg Wilson
45 Greg Wilson
46 Greg Wilson
47 Greg Wilson
48 Greg Wilson
49 Greg Wilson
50 (top) Peter Margonelli
50 (bottom) Steven Brooke
51 Peter Margonelli
52 Dennis Krukowski
53 Dennis Krukowski
54 Dennis Krukowski
55 Dennis Krukowski
56 Dennis Krukowski
57 Dennis Krukowski
58 Dennis Krukowski
59 Dennis Krukowski
60 Dennis Krukowski
61 Dennis Krukowski
62 Dennis Krukowski
63 Dennis Krukowski

64 Sargent Architectural Photography
65 Sargent Architectural Photography
66 Sargent Architectural Photography
67 Sargent Architectural Photography

DEEP SOUTH

page:

76 Greg Campbell Photography
77 Greg Campbell Photography
78 Emily Minton
79 Emily Minton
80 Emily Minton
81 Emily Minton
82 (top) Bill Holt
82 (bottom) Tom Joynt
83 Rick Taylor
84 Gordon Beall
85 Gordon Beall
86 (top) Gordon Beall
86 (bottom) Bill Holt
87 Gordon Beall
88 Barry Fikes
89 Barry Fikes
90 Barry Fikes
91 Barry Fikes
92 Dennis Krukowski
93 Dennis Krukowski
94 Keith Carey
95 Keith Carey
96 Chris Little
97 Chris Little
98 (top) Keith Carey
98 (bottom) Chris Little
99 Keith Carey
100 Dikeman
101 Dikeman
102 Chipper Hatter
108 (top) Pat Shanklin
108 (bottom) Robert Starling
109 Pat Shanklin
110 Robert Starling
111 Pat Shanklin
116 Emily Minton
117 Emily Minton
118 Emily Minton
119 Emily Minton
120 Double Image Studios
121 Double Image Studios
122 Double Image Studios
123 Double Image Studios

NEW SOUTH

page:

126 Dennis Krukowski
127 Dennis Krukowski
128 Rob Muir
129 John Blackmer
130 Rob Muir
131 John Blackmer
132 Atelier Wong Photography
133 Atelier Wong Photography
134 Atelier Wong Photography
135 Atelier Wong Photography
136 Tina Weitz Photography
137 Tine Weitz Photography
144 Colleen Duffley
145 Colleen Duffley
146 Emily Minton
147 Emily Minton
148 Colleen Duffley
149 Colleen Duffley
150 Jack Weigler
151 Jack Weigler
152 Jack Weigler
153 Jack Weigler

Ann Carter Inc.
11 East Hill Drive
Jackson, MS 39216
601/981.5820
601/366.6578 fax

Annelle Primos & Associates
4500 I-55 North
Suite 126
Jackson, MS 39211
601/362.6154
601/362.0733 fax

Benjamin Noriega-Ortiz
75 Spring Street
New York, NY 10012
212/343.9709
212/343.9263 fax

C. Weaks Interiors
3391 Habersham Road
Atlanta, GA 30305
404/233.6040
404/233.6043 fax

Charme Tate Interiors
1437 Old Square Road, Suite 107
Jackson, MS 39211
601/981.5589
601/981.2409 fax

Cheryl A. Van Duyne, ASID Interior
Designer
14999 Preston Road
Suite 215
Dallas, TX 75248
972/387.3070
972/385.1169

Clements Antiques of Florida
9501 US Highway 98 West
Destin, FL 32541
850/837.1473
850/654.4562 fax

Crawford's Interior Design
221 East Kings Way
Winter Park, FL 32789
407/628.3939
407/628.2375 fax

Danny Hartley Interiors, Inc.
1653 North McFaraland Boulevard
Tuscaloosa, AL 35406
205/345.9578
205/345.9565 fax

David Holcomb Interiors
2188 Bohler Road NW
Atlanta, GA 30327-1136
404/355.0543
404/355.0543 fax

Design Effects
P. O. Box 7005
Boca Raton, FL 33431
561/392.6301
561/395.4409 fax

Design House
200 Westcott
Houston, TX 77007
713/803.4949
713/803.4950 fax

G. S. Hinsen Company
2133 Bandywood Drive
Nashville, TN 37215
615/383.6440
615/269.5130 fax

Ginny Stine Interiors
1936 San Marco Boulevard
Jacksonville, FL 32207
904/396.9814
904/398.3175 fax

Jack Fhillips Design, Inc.
7 Via Parigi
Palm Beach, FL 33480
561/659.4459
561/659.0949 fax

Jane Page Creative Designs
200 Westcott
Houston, TX 77007
713/803.4999
713/803.4998 fax

Jo Emmert Interior Design
6033 Esplanade Avenue
Baton Rouge, LA 70806
504/923.1907
504/927.9793 fax

Landy Gardner Interiors
2212 Bandywood Drive
Nashville, TN 37215
615/383.1880
615/383.4167 fax

Leo Dowell Interiors, Inc.
501 East Morehead Street
Suite #2
Charlotte, NC 28202
704/334.3817
704/334.5830 fax

Linda McCalla Interiors
604 South Church Street
Georgetown, TX 78626
512/930.9987
512/869.0666 fax

Linda Poletti Interior Decoration
2901 Washington Road
West Palm Beach, FL 33405
561/659.4704
561/659.1595 fax

Lovelace Interiors
12870 US Highway 98 West
Destin, FL 32541
850/837.5563
850/654.5867 fax

Marc-Michaels Interior Design
300 Park Avenue South
Winter Park, FL 32789

Myrl Talkington Designs
6915 Tokalon
Dallas, TX 75214
214/321.1199
214/321.4067 fax

Pedlar's Village Interior Design
3562 South Osprey Avenue
Sarasota, FL 34239
941/955.5726
941/366.9563 fax

Piano Nobile
233 Aragon Avenue
Coral Gables, FL 33134
305/444.0528
305/444.0842 fax

Retro Interiors, Inc.
1483 North Federal Highway
Fort Lauderdale, FL 33304
954/561.1058
954/561.4890 fax

Rod Mickley Interior Design
3240 Cardinal Drive
Suite 102
Vero Beach, FL 32963
561/234.4550
561/234.5290 fax

Rogers-Ford Architecture Interior Design
2616 Thomas Avenue
Dallas, TX 75204
214/871.9388
214/871.3155 fax

Sanford R. Thigpen, Interiors, Inc.
2996 Grandview Avenue NE
Suite 310
Atlanta, GA 30305
404/351.1411
404/240.0558

Spectrum Interior Design
6000 North AIA
Vero Beach, FL 32963
561/234.4427
561/231.4166 fax

Swann Interiors
241 Country Club Road
Macon, GA 31210
912/477.7803

Yoggy Crow, Inc.
330 Oak Lane
Richmond, VA
804/359.6429
804/358.3985 fax

Atelier Wong Photography
1009 East 40th Street
Suite 100
Austin, TX 78751
512/371.1288
512/371.1288 fax

Greg Campbell Photography
352 East Northside Drive
Jackson, MS 39206

Judi Davis
P. O. Box 10533
Jacksonville, FL 32247-0533

Double Image Studio
804/232.5500

Jack Gardner
Jack Gardner Photography
P. O. Box 7
Valpraiso, FL 32580
850/678.7702
850/729.1331 fax

Dennis Krukowski
329 East 92 Street
Suite 1D
New York, NY 10128
212/860.0912
212/860.0913 fax

Emily Minton
Emily Minton Photography
P. O. Box 77462
Atlanta, GA 30357
404/355.8818
404/355.8818 fax

Sargent Architectural Photography
4123 Burns Road
Palm Beach Gardens, FL 33410
407/627.4711
407/627.4790 fax

David Schilling
Schilling Photography
1816 D Briarwood Ind. Court
Atlanta, GA 30329
404/636.1399
770/582.0972 fax

Robert Starling Photography
Orlando, FL
407/521.0041

Laurence F. Taylor
Orlando, FL
407/897.2005

Tina Weitz
Tina Weitz Photography
1748 Ohlen Road #3
Austin, TX 78757-7860
512/323.5851
512/323.5071 fax